HAPPINESS
IS NOT A
DESTINATION.
IT IS A
WAY
OF LIFE.

50 CENT
MOUSTACHE
RIDES

# COOK LIKE A MAN

# CHANGING THE FACE OF MEN'S HEALTH

The Mo (slang for moustache) and Movember come together each year in November, a month-long charity event which brings the moustache back to raise awareness for men's health.

Once registered at movember.com each Mo Bro must begin the 1st of Movember with a clean-shaven face. For the entire month they must grow and groom a moustache. There is to be no joining of the Mo to the sideburns (that's considered a beard), there's to be no joining of the handlebars to the chin (that's considered a goatee) and each Mo Bro must conduct himself like a true gentleman.

Mo Bros effectively become walking talking billboards for the 30 days of November and through their actions and words raise funds and awareness by prompting private and public conversation around the often ignored issue of men's health. A Mo Sista is a woman who loves a Mo; an individual who is dedicated to supporting the Mo Bros in her life and their moustache-growing efforts.

Since way back in 2003, more than 3.05 million Mo Bros and Mo Sistas have got behind the moustache. In 2012, £90.5 million (€112 million) was raised globally and in 2013 there are campaigns in 21 countries across the globe. Join us as we stand tall and help change the face of men's health.

THE OFFICIAL MOVEMBER COOKBOOK

# COOK LIKE A MAN

*The ultimate cookbook for
the modern gentleman*

— **MOVEMBER** —

**B⬦XTREE**

FIRST PUBLISHED 2013 BY BOXTREE
an imprint of Pan Macmillan, a division of
Macmillan Publishers Limited
Pan Macmillan,
20 New Wharf Road, London N1 9RR
Basingstoke and Oxford
Associated companies throughout the world
**www.panmacmillan.com**

ISBN 978-0-7522-6553-7

Original design by Movember
Photography by Steve Ryan/steveryanphotography.com
*Cook Like a Man* project edited by Emma Marriott
*Cook Like a Man* designed and typeset by Lucy Parissi
Printed and bound in China

Visit **www.panmacmillan.com** to read more about all
our books and to buy them. You will also find features,
author interviews and news of any author events, and
you can sign up for e-newsletters so that you're always
first to hear about our new releases.

# CONTENTS

INTRODUCTION                                    6
GOOD EATING                                     8
ESSENTIAL TOOLS                                10
TIPS FOR THE KITCHEN                            12
A GENTLEMAN'S PANTRY                           14

COOK SOUPS AND SALADS                          16
COOK STARTERS AND SMALL DISHES                 42
COOK BARBECUES                                 70
COOK MEAT                                      88
COOK GASTRONOMIC TRAILBLAZERS                 108
COOK POULTRY AND GAME                         122
COOK FISH                                     134
COOK DESSERTS                                 158
COOK SAUCES, CHUTNEYS AND JAMS                178

THE PERSONA OF A MAN WITH A MO                184
INDEX                                         186
MOUSTACHE RESPECT                             190

'A GENTLEMAN IS ALWAYS
A GIVER. GIVING OF
TIME, KNOWLEDGE AND
TECHNIQUES – ESPECIALLY
A GOOD RECIPE'

# INTRODUCTION

Around the globe men have joined together each November to stand tall with their fellow men and grow a moustache to raise funds and awareness for men's health.

A Mo Bro – as a participant of this prestigious event is known – is a strong, confident individual. He has a love of life and a lot of living to do. He is a leader of men. He can run a company, design a building, fix a gearbox, or replace a boiler, but sadly some Mo Bros can't boil an egg.

Enter the Mo Bro Chef – a purveyor of knowledge, moustaches and a good meal. In pursuit of the preservation of the time-honoured tradition of good eating, the Mo Bro Chef has evolved from a 'gas mark 2' greenhorn to fearless gourmand.

The time has come for regular Mo's to stand alongside these Mo Bro Chefs and summon the collective wisdom and experience of the culinary greats. The time has come for a cookbook, a real cookbook with real recipes – from serious salads and soups to a host of meat, fish and poultry dishes, gastronomic trailblazers and barbecues – all from some of the best Mo Bro Chefs in the land.

Here you'll find tips and recipes inspired by cuisines from around the world: spices, herbs and our little friend who packs a mean punch, the chilli, make frequent appearances in this collection of Mo-friendly recipes.

So close that microwave door, put on an apron, pick up those tongs, come together with your Mo Bros and Mo Sistas, and cook like a man.

# GOOD EATING

There are many things that would make our lives a whole lot better if we could control them – the economy, the rain when you've organised a barbecue, disappearing socks … you know the sort of thing.

But one thing we can control is our diet, exercise and knowing what makes us tick. It's something we can actively manage to improve our health – from reducing the risk of things such as diabetes and heart disease, to getting to know personal health indicators such as cholesterol levels and family health history.

Simple things such as getting off the bus one stop earlier, or walking upstairs rather than using the lift, combined with other forms of exercise can all be of benefit in a Mo Bro's daily routine.

Getting your 'five a day' of fruit and vegetables is no doubt a good idea for improving diet and your health in general, and tomatoes contain a plant chemical called lycopene, which may slow down the growth of prostate cancer. Cooked and processed tomatoes, such as tomato sauces, soups, purées and pastes, are a better source of lycopene than fresh tomatoes. While the tomato is one of the kings of the lycopene world, the antioxidant can also be found in watermelons, pink grapefruits, guavas and papayas.

So when you are planning a Mo Bro feast that centres on fish, meat or beast, remember to balance the meal with plenty of vegetables and maybe even some cooked tomatoes – recipes for which you will find aplenty in *Cook Like a Man*.

'GOOD KNIVES ARE YOUR BEST FRIEND IN THE KITCHEN, PAY A LITTLE MORE FOR QUALITY AND DON'T LET ANYONE ELSE SHARPEN THEM'

# ESSENTIAL TOOLS

1 – Sharp knives. Invest in a quality blade of German or Japanese make. Purchase a whetstone, learn how to maintain the cutting edge and keep it razor sharp. These cost a little more but will last a lifetime. Never let anyone sharpen, use or touch your blade.

2 – A full set of stainless steel pots and saucepans. Various sizes and no plastic handles. A stock pot is a must for making soups and stocks. A cast iron stew pot, at least 20cm in diameter, will last a lifetime and you can cook just about anything in them from Bolognese to lamb shanks.

3 – Hand blender. An invaluable tool for sauces, soups, smoothies, margaritas and just about anything that you need to purée.

4 – Mandolin vegetable slicer. An essential instrument that will have you preparing vegetables and garnishes like a pro. Be warned – it's also responsible for more cuts in the kitchen than any other implement.

5 – Espresso 'mocha' pot. Bialetti brand. Forget about the expensive coffee machines, these cost about £30 and, along with a saucepan of warm milk, make a perfect coffee. The fact that every Italian household has one of these should tell you that this is all you'll ever need.

6 – Microplane. For zesting citrus fruits and spices for that something extra.

7 – Blowtorch. It makes fire. Enough said.

8 – Speed peeler. There are peelers and then there are peelers. This is the latter. Great for making ribbons of cucumber, carrot, parmesan and makes peeling potatoes simple.

9 – A good-quality frying pan. Heavy-bottomed so it retains heat and cooks food quickly and properly by transferring heat effectively.

10 – Scales and measuring jugs. Many recipes, especially pastries, call for exact amounts so no cowboys please.

11 – Chopping boards. Get a large, heavy wooden board – it will cost a little more but also last a lifetime. A plastic chopping board is also good to have on hand for chicken and fish.

12 – Liquidiser. You'll be amazed how many things you can blitz. Mealshake, anyone?

13 – Food processor. It dices, it slices, it mows the lawn.

14 – A set of three oven roasting trays.

15 – Meat thermometer. If you're cooking a roast, this inexpensive tool will have you cooking your meat to a perfect temperature.

16 – For barbecues: extra-long tongs, liquid barbecue fuel, charcoal, 'stubbie' holders (beer cooler).

# TIPS FOR THE KITCHEN

- Start cooking with a clean kitchen. Empty the bins and clear the bench tops, you'll need the space. Professional chefs start their nightly service with a spotless kitchen, so should you – things are going to get messy. Also, where possible, clean as you go – waking up to a bombsite kitchen after a big night is never good.

- Try to buy tomatoes 'on the vine' and in season. Never store in the fridge – instead let them continue to ripen in your fruit bowl.

- Always remove your steaks from the fridge 30 minutes before you are going to cook. This allows the meat to warm to room temperature which will leave it relaxed and soft – ready to be cooked.

- Use a hot pan to cook your fish crispy and your steak juicy.

- Don't get stressed. A Mo Bro is measured and in complete control.

- Always be good to your mother. Always.

## BUYING FRESH FISH AND OYSTERS

- When buying fresh fish or oysters talk to your fishmonger – tell them what you're planning on cooking and ask their advice. Fishmongers and butchers enjoy a customer with passion for the food they sell.

- How to tell how fresh fish is? Look for bright, bulging eyes. When lightly pressed, the flesh of fresh fish should be quite resilient and bounce back. The older it gets the more likely it is that the indent will remain or slowly bounce back.

- It should of course smell fresh; the more it smells like 'fish' the older it is. The fresher it is the less unpleasant aroma there will be. Fish should smell of the sea.

## STERILISING JARS AND BOTTLES

- Any sauces, chutneys or man jams that you make need to be stored in sterilised jars or bottles. It's best to prepare them in advance so they're ready and waiting to be filled.

- Thoroughly wash new and used jars in hot soapy water. Then either put the upturned jars on a baking sheet and heat in a preheated oven for 10–15 minutes at 150°C/gas mark 2. Or run the upturned jars through a hot dishwasher cycle.

# A GENTLEMAN'S PANTRY

A Mo Bro Chef should always have the following ingredients in his cupboards:

- Anchovies
- Baby oil
- Balsamic vinegar
- Capers
- Chocolate body paint
- Coconut milk
- Couscous
- Extra-virgin olive oil
- Flour
- Garlic
- HP sauce
- Mustard
- Noodles
- Olives
- Onions
- Pasta
- Peppercorns
- Plum tomatoes
- Porcini
- Rice
- Sea salt flakes
- Spanish paprika
- Sugar
- Vegetable bouillon powder
- White wine vinegar
- Wine – red and white
- Worcestershire sauce

Make time to source the best ingredients you can find. A trip to a bustling farmers' market will give you the chance to talk to suppliers and find inspiration. Our distinct seasons provide a constantly changing smorgasbord of produce – get involved.

JANUARY AND FEBRUARY
Purple-sprouting broccoli, beetroot and parsnips. Guinea fowl and rabbit.

MARCH AND APRIL
Kale and Jerusalem artichokes. Jersey royal potatoes.

MAY AND JUNE
Asparagus, artichokes and broad beans. Spring lamb.

JULY AND AUGUST
Strawberries, raspberries and blueberries. Courgettes and figs. Scallops and monkfish.

SEPTEMBER AND OCTOBER
Plums, apples and pears. Partridge and venison.

MOVEMBER AND DECEMBER
Brussel sprouts, celeriac and leeks. Pheasant, guinea fowl and rabbit.

## FOODS TO APPROACH WITH CAUTION WHEN SPORTING A NEW MOUSTACHE

1. Cappuccino
2. Glass of milk
3. Irish cream ale, stout
4. Joints of mutton
5. Milkshake
6. Candyfloss
7. Chocolate cannoli
8. Spaghetti carbonara
9. Meat pie (when eaten with hands)
10. Lamb kebab
11. Tacos
12. Singapore crab

# COOK
# SOUPS AND SALADS

# VINE TOMATO AND PLUM SOUP WITH BRAZIL NUT AND PUMPKIN SEED LOAF

**DAVE BONE**

## SERVES 8

2kg vine plum tomatoes
6 Victoria plums
4 basil stalks and leaves
4 banana shallots
3 garlic cloves
50ml extra-virgin olive oil, plus
a drizzle for serving
25ml Merlot vinegar
700ml vegetable stock
Basil leaves to serve
Salt and pepper

Preheat the oven to 150˚C/gas mark 2. Cut the tomatoes and plums in half, remove the stones from the plums, and place on a baking tray with the basil. Bake in the oven for around 1 hour or until they start to wrinkle.

Peel and chop the shallots and garlic, then place in a heavy-bottomed pan with the olive oil. Fry slowly until soft, being careful not to let them colour.

Add the vinegar, reduce by half, then add the vegetable stock and bring to a simmer. Add the tomatoes and plums to the stock. Boil for 5 minutes and then take off the heat and leave to infuse for 10 minutes.

Place the soup in a liquidiser or blender, and blitz until smooth. Season to taste. Serve in a bowl with a drizzle of oil and basil leaves.

# BRAZIL NUT AND PUMPKIN SEED LOAF

1 teaspoon sugar
1 teaspoon dried yeast or
15g fresh yeast
110g brown flour
110g strong white flour
1 teaspoon salt
80g roasted Brazil nuts,
chopped
10g roasted pumpkin seeds,
plus 5g for sprinkling on
top of loaf
20g butter for greasing
1 egg yolk

Dissolve the sugar and yeast in 150ml warm water and leave for 10 minutes.

Slowly combine the liquid with the brown and strong white flours, add the salt, and mix until you have a soft dough. Then mix in the chopped Brazil nuts and 10g pumpkin seeds.

Knead by hand on a lightly floured surface for 5–10 minutes until you have a smooth dough. Then shape into a loaf before placing in a well-greased loaf tin. Place a polythene bag over the tin and tie loosely. Leave until the dough doubles in size.

Preheat the oven to 200˚C/gas mark 6. Remove the dough from the bag, brush the top with egg yolk and sprinkle on the remaining pumpkin seeds. Bake in the oven for 30–40 minutes, or until golden and risen and the base sounds hollow when tapped.

# CAULIFLOWER SOUP WITH SHERRY TAPENADE

### RICHARD ROBINSON

## SERVES 6

1 cauliflower
1 litre semi-skimmed milk
Salt and pepper

## SHERRY TAPENADE

1 garlic clove, peeled and
chopped
100g black olives, pitted
Zest and juice of ¼ lemon
2 anchovies, chopped
A small handful of chopped
parsley
Sweet sherry to taste
Extra-virgin olive oil

Thinly slice the cauliflower, place in a saucepan with the milk and slowly bring to the point of boiling. Turn down the heat and cook for a further 5 minutes or until the cauliflower is soft.

Place in a blender and blend until smooth. Season to taste. Refrigerate until ready to use. This soup can be served chilled or hot.

## FOR THE SHERRY TAPENADE

In a food processor, whiz the garlic, olives, lemon zest and juice, anchovies and parsley to a paste, then mix in enough sherry to taste. Store covered in the fridge.

## TO SERVE

Place a spoonful of the tapenade on top of the soup or on a thin slice of griddled baguette and add a drizzle of olive oil. Serve with some crusty bread.

'COOKING IS LIKE LOVE. IT SHOULD BE ENTERED INTO WITH ABANDON OR NOT AT ALL'

HARRIET VAN HORNE

# SPICY TOMATO AND RED PEPPER SOUP, SEARED PRAWNS, OLIVE OIL AND CHIVES

**SAM WILSON**

## SERVES 4

3 red peppers, halved
4 plum tomatoes
4 tablespoons olive oil
2 small red onions, peeled and chopped
2 garlic cloves, peeled and chopped
1 tablespoon ground cumin
2 teaspoons paprika
1 large potato, peeled and chopped
2 x 400g cans chopped tomatoes
500ml vegetable stock
Salt and pepper

## TO SERVE

12 Saudi (or large) prawns
1 red chilli, deseeded and chopped
½ bunch of chives, finely chopped
150g crème fraîche
A drizzle of good olive oil
Fresh pesto (optional)

Preheat the oven to 220°C/gas mark 7. Put the peppers and plum tomatoes on a roasting tray and drizzle over half the olive oil. Roast in the oven until slightly charred and softened.

Meanwhile, in a large saucepan, cook the onions and garlic in the remaining olive oil until softened. Add the cumin and paprika, and cook until the aromas start to come out.

Add the potato, tinned tomatoes, stock and roasted tomatoes, and cook on a low heat for about 45 minutes.

Transfer to a blender and whizz (you may need to do this in batches), then pass through a sieve to remove any bits. The soup should be nice and fragrant with a touch of sweetness. Season to taste. You may need to reheat in a saucepan.

## TO SERVE

In a separate frying pan, sear the prawns in a little oil, chilli and seasoning until they are just cooked. Mix the chives into the crème fraîche. Pour the soup into warm bowls. Gently place the prawns on the soup so they don't sink, and garnish with the crème fraîche, a drizzle of olive oil and fresh pesto.

# CHILLED WATERCRESS SOUP, PRAWNS, CHILLI CRÈME FRAÎCHE

**DEON JANSEN**

Watercress is a semi-aquatic perennial and one of the oldest-known leaf vegetables to be consumed by human beings. It is rich in minerals and iron, and very easy to find, making it a great item to forage if you're hoping to impress a lady with your survival skills in the great outdoors.

## SERVES 6

1 onion, diced
2 garlic cloves, peeled and crushed
25ml olive oil
2 potatoes, peeled and diced
400ml good-quality vegetable stock
1 vegetable stock cube
300g watercress, plus a little extra to serve
Salt and pepper

## TO SERVE

30 medium prawns, peeled
Red amaranth (or any micro leaves)
200ml crème fraîche
1 red chilli, deseeded and diced

Chill 6 serving bowls in the fridge. In a heavy-bottomed saucepan, slowly fry the onion and garlic in the olive oil until translucent. Add the diced potato, vegetable stock and stock cube and gently bring to the boil.

Turn down the temperature and cook gently until the potato is tender. Transfer to a plastic container and place in the fridge to chill completely.

Place the watercress in a blender and pour in the chilled vegetable stock and potatoes. Add a pinch of salt and pepper and blend until very smooth.

## TO SERVE

Remove the bowls from the fridge and add in the cold soup. Top each soup with 5 prawns and a small bundle of red amaranth (or any micro leaves will do). Fill 6 side dishes with crème fraîche and sprinkle with the diced chilli. Arrange the soup, crème fraîche and a little extra watercress on a serving plate or wooden board, and serve.

'COOKERY HAS BECOME
A NOBLE ART, A NOBLE SCIENCE;
COOKS ARE GENTLEMEN'

**DEON JANSEN**

# THAI BEEF SALAD

## BRAD STOWARD

### SERVES 6

30g Thai jasmine rice
50ml kecap manis sweet soy sauce
300g beef sirloin

### SALAD

2 spring onions, finely sliced
300g Chinese leaves, finely sliced
20g coriander leaves
20g mint leaves
2 shallots, finely sliced
1 long red chilli, deseeded and sliced

### DRESSING

100ml lime juice
10g chilli powder
50ml fish sauce
3 bird's eye chillies, finely sliced
60ml sweet chilli sauce

Heat a dry frying pan, add the rice and toss continuously until it has turned golden brown. Then put the rice in a mortar and pestle or a blender and pound or blitz until it is a fine powder (you can make a large batch of this and keep in an airtight container for weeks).

Combine all the ingredients for the dressing and mix well. It should be hot, sour, salty and slightly sweet. Set aside until serving.

Toss all the salad ingredients together in a bowl and set aside until serving. (Do not dress the salad until serving).

Rub the soy sauce all over the beef and marinate for 10 minutes. Heat a griddle pan until hot, then cook the beef for 2½ minutes each side for rare, 4 minutes each side for medium. Transfer to a board and rest for 5 minutes.

### TO SERVE

Slice the beef across the grain into thin slices and toss with the salad, adding any juices. Add the dressing and toss thoroughly, and arrange the salad on a large serving plate. Sprinkle the roasted rice powder over the top for extra crunch. Serve immediately.

# GRILLED MACKEREL, NIÇOISE SALAD, LEMON AND CHIVE DRESSING

**SAM WILSON**

Oily fish such as mackerel, sardines, fresh tuna and salmon are easy to prepare and high in Omega 3, an essential fatty acid.

## SERVES 4

2 red peppers
200g new potatoes
200g green beans
3 eggs
1 punnet red cherry tomatoes, cut into quarters
2 shallots, peeled and sliced
80g pitted Kalamata olives
¼ bunch of parsley, chopped
Zest of 1 lemon
4 mackerel, butterflied by the fishmonger
Salt and pepper
Olive oil for frying

## DRESSING

Juice of 2 lemons
80ml olive oil
1 tablespoon Dijon mustard
A bunch of chives, chopped

## FOR THE SALAD

Preheat the oven to 220°C/gas mark 7. Place the red peppers in the oven and roast until the skin blisters. Remove the peppers from the oven, cover with cling film and allow to sweat. Once cooled, the skin should peel off easily. Remove the seeds, slice and set aside.

Cook the new potatoes in boiling water until tender. Cool, cut into quarters and set aside. Blanch the green beans in salted boiling water for 1 minute or until al dente, then cool in iced water, drain and set aside.

Bring a pan of water to the boil, then add the eggs and cook for 5–6 minutes. Place the eggs in cold water to cool, then remove their shells, slice into quarters and set aside.

Put the tomatoes, shallots, olives, chopped parsley and lemon zest in a bowl. Add the rest of the salad ingredients, except the eggs, and mix together. In a separate bowl, mix together all the dressing ingredients and put to one side.

## FOR THE MACKEREL

Put a non-stick pan on a medium heat and add a little olive oil. Season the mackerel, place in the pan and cook until the skin is golden brown. Flip over and do the same for the other side. This should take 4–5 minutes to cook.

## TO SERVE

Mix the dressing with the salad and put on a plate. Place the mackerel on top with the egg wedges as a garnish.

# RAW BEEF, CAPERS, CHICORY AND PICKLED WALNUTS

**FRED SMITH**

## SERVES 6

1.2kg fresh bavette steak, finely chopped
Sea salt
6 egg yolks
Plenty of grilled sourdough bread to serve

## SALAD

3 heads of chicory (endive)
300g watercress
1 large shallot, peeled and finely sliced
6 pickled walnuts, sliced
100g capers (extra fine if possible)

## DRESSING

2 tablespoons Dijon mustard
2 teaspoons good-quality red wine vinegar
2 teaspoons vinegar from the pickled walnuts
300ml extra-virgin olive oil

To make the dressing, mix the mustard with the vinegars and slowly whisk in the olive oil to create a smooth dressing.

For the salad, separate the chicory leaves and roughly slice, mix with the watercress, shallot, walnuts and capers.

Season the beef with salt to taste and divide between six plates. Place an egg yolk in the middle of the beef. Mix in the dressing with the salad and serve on the side with hot grilled sourdough.

# WARM PIGEON BREAST SALAD WITH CARAMELISED APPLE, CRISPY CHORIZO AND BALSAMIC SYRUP

**ANDY WAUGH AND RUARIDH EMSLIE**

## SERVES 6

6 pigeon breasts
3 Cox's eating apples
100ml balsamic vinegar
3 tablespoons brown sugar
A knob of butter
200g thinly sliced chorizo
300g salad leaves
Salt and pepper

Remove the pigeon breasts from the fridge and warm to room temperature. Core the apples, keeping their skin on, and cut into 8 thin wedges.

Heat the balsamic vinegar and sugar in a small saucepan over a medium heat, stirring until the sugar dissolves. Then leave to bubble gently for about 15 minutes until reduced by a half. Add more sugar or vinegar to taste.

In a pan, melt a knob of butter on a low heat and add the apple slices. Cook the apples slowly on each side until golden in colour. The natural sugars in the apple will caramelise and sweeten the apple. Remove and keep warm.

Season the pigeon breasts and add to the pan that you cooked the apples in. Cook on a medium-to-high heat for 2 minutes on each side until medium rare. Remove from the pan, allow to rest and slice each breast into 5 pieces. Keep the pan on the heat and add the sliced chorizo, cooking for 30 seconds each side until crisp.

### TO SERVE

Place a pile of salad leaves on each plate and put the pigeon on top. Drizzle the warm balsamic syrup over the breast and salad. Then add the apple wedges and chorizo on top.

'AT A DINNER PARTY ONE SHOULD EAT WISELY BUT NOT TOO WELL, AND TALK WELL BUT NOT TOO WISELY...'

W. SOMERSET MAUGHAM

# SOM TAM GREEN PAPAYA SALAD

### BRAD STOWARD

This salad is a staple of Thai cuisine.

## SERVES 2

3 garlic cloves, peeled
A pinch of salt
2–4 bird's eye chillies, deseeded
and chopped
1 heaped tablespoon crushed
roasted peanuts
2 tablespoons dried prawns
1 tablespoon lime juice
4 cherry tomatoes, quartered
4 fine green beans
1 green papaya, peeled
2 tablespoons palm sugar
1–2 tablespoons fish sauce

In a large pestle and mortar, pound the garlic with the salt and chillies. Add the peanuts and dried prawns, and pound into a coarse paste. Add the lime juice, cherry tomatoes and green beans, and gently mash together.

Julienne the papaya by slicing it lengthways and cutting it into matchsticks. Add the papaya to the mortar and bruise it gently.

Tip everything into a bowl, and mix in the palm sugar, lime juice and fish sauce.

# GET TOGETHER

*'A well-groomed moustache is the key to many great outfits and an essential ingredient at a Movember dinner party. No Mo – no go.'*

Cooking at home should be an enjoyable, rewarding exercise that can bring family, friends, food and conversation together around the table. But the words 'dinner party' can strike fear in the home cook. For some, it is an opportunity to invite friends round and lord it over their captive guests on home turf, owning the night as learned sommelier, DJ, host with the most and chef de cuisine. For others, it means days of planning and slaving over a hot stove in an attempt to impress friends with non-existent skills, only to go down in flames when the night arrives.

The 'perfect' dinner party brings to mind magical evenings of social grandeur. The impeccably dressed host greeting guests at the door, champagne and canapés on arrival, seamless courses of Michelin star-worthy haute cuisine and conversation so significant that it actually means something. Rubbish. This cookbook is for Mo Bros and Mo Sistas and they, more than anyone, understand that any home-cooked meal shared with friends makes for a great night.

So invite your friends round, make a glorious mess, cook up a storm and let the good times roll.

# POACHED TROUT, HERB SALAD AND MAYONNAISE

**GILES CLARK**

## SERVES 6

A 1.5kg whole trout, cleaned and scaled
Salt
2 bottles of white wine
1 fennel bulb, sliced
2 garlic bulbs
2 lemons

250g reduced-fat mayonnaise
½ bunch of parsley
½ bunch of dill
½ bunch of chives
Extra-virgin olive oil
2 large crusty baguettes to serve

Season the trout with salt inside and out. Fill a large pan with the wine, 1.5 litres water, the fennel and garlic. Simmer for 30 minutes to infuse the flavours.

Add the trout – if your pan isn't big enough, cut the fish in half. Turn down the heat so it's just below a boil, and gently poach the fish for 20–30 minutes. The fish is cooked when the flesh next to the spine comes away from the bone easily.

Squeeze the juice from the lemons and stir through the mayonnaise in a bowl. Pick the parsley and dill, and chop the chives into 2.5cm batons. Lightly toss the herbs in a bowl with a dash of olive oil.

## TO SERVE

Carefully remove the fish from the liquid and serve whole in the middle of the table with the mayonnaise, herbs and crusty bread.

# COOK
# STARTERS AND SMALL DISHES

# SPICED CRAB AND AVOCADO ON TOAST

**DAVID JOHNSON**

## SERVES 6

2 red chillies
½ bunch of coriander
400g white crab meat
3 lemons
100ml extra-virgin olive oil
3 ripe green avocados
2 garlic cloves
1 loaf sourdough bread
2 bunches of watercress
Salt and pepper

Deseed the red chillies and finely chop with the coriander. In a bowl, flake the crab meat and add the chopped coriander and chilli. Zest one of the lemons, squeeze the juice of half a lemon and add to the crab meat with 25ml of the olive oil. Season to taste and place in the fridge until needed.

Peel and remove the stones from the avocados. Place in a food processor with the juice of half a lemon, the garlic and the remainder of the oil. Blend until smooth.

Slice the sourdough into thick slices and grill both sides on a griddle pan until well toasted. Spread the avocado purée over, then spoon the crab meat on top. Drizzle with a little oil, top with watercress and serve with wedges of lemon.

**'MAN SHALL NOT LIVE
BY BREAD ALONE'**

**THE BIBLE**

# WILD MUSHROOM CAPPUCCINO, WILD MUSHROOM CROUSTADES

## RICHARD ROBINSON

You could forage for your mushrooms but a Mo Bro should only undertake this with absolute knowledge of what he is doing. Pick and eat only the fungi you are certain are safe for consumption and double check with an expert.

### SERVES 6

### MUSHROOM CAPPUCCINO

A knob of unsalted butter
300g mixed wild mushrooms, such as chanterelles or morels, cleaned and sliced
4 round shallots, peeled and finely sliced
150g celery, finely diced
2 garlic cloves, peeled and crushed
Salt and freshly cracked black pepper
200ml Madeira
500ml chicken stock
200ml double cream

### CROUSTADES

6 large 1cm-thick slices plain brioche (available from good delicatessens)
A knob of unsalted butter
1 tablespoon olive oil
500g mixed wild mushrooms, cleaned and sliced
1 garlic clove, peeled and crushed
1 banana shallot, peeled and sliced into thin rings
Salt and cracked black pepper
1 teaspoon chopped fresh thyme
A few sprigs of chervil

### FOR THE MUSHROOM CAPPUCCINO

In a large saucepan, heat the butter gently until it starts to foam. Add the mushrooms, sliced shallots, diced celery, crushed garlic and seasoning. Sauté until golden in colour. Add the Madeira, bring it to the boil and then simmer until the Madeira is reduced by half.

Pour in the chicken stock, reduce the heat, and gently simmer for about 20 minutes. Add the cream and simmer gently for a further 5 minutes – do not boil the soup as the cream will split. Transfer the soup to a blender and blitz until very smooth and frothy. Set aside until serving.

### FOR THE CROUSTADES

Toast the brioche slices until golden brown on both sides. Using a cookie cutter, cut 3 circles out of each brioche slice. Heat a large non-stick frying pan and add the butter and oil.

As soon as the butter starts to foam, add the mushrooms, garlic, shallots and seasoning, and sauté until golden brown. When the mushrooms are cooked, add the chopped fresh thyme and divide the mixture between the toasted croustades. Top each with a sprig of chervil.

### TO SERVE

Gently reheat the soup. For extra cappuccino foam, return the soup to a deep saucepan and use a hand blender to aerate it further. The soup must be hot as it aerates best if the temperature is just below boiling point. If the soup is too thick it will not foam so add a dash of chicken stock to thin it down slightly if necessary. Serve the cappuccinos in 6 small bowls or espresso cups with the croustades on the side.

# BAKED CHEESE WITH WINTER HERBS

## LUCA & GUGLIELMO D'ALFONSO

### SERVES 6

300g wheel of Gubbeen cheese
(or similar soft cheese)
1 tablespoon chopped fresh
herbs, such as thyme and
rosemary
2 garlic cloves, peeled and
chopped
A pinch of cracked black
pepper
A loaf of crusty bread

Preheat the oven to 160°C/gas mark 3. Cut the cheese in half horizontally to make two rounds. Sprinkle the herbs, garlic and black pepper on the bottom half of the cheese. Replace the top disc of cheese and place the wheel on a large piece of tin foil.

Wrap the foil around the cheese, forming a chimney hole on top with the excess foil so moisture can escape while the cheese bakes. Place the cheese on a baking sheet and bake for 20 minutes, or until the cheese is soft and runny.

### TO SERVE

Spread on slices of chunky bread and eat while the cheese is still warm.

'ONE OF THE NICEST THINGS ABOUT
LIFE IS THE WAY WE MUST
REGULARLY STOP WHATEVER IT IS
WE ARE DOING AND DEVOTE OUR
ATTENTION TO EATING'

**LUCIANO PAVAROTTI**

# 'THE BELLY RULES THE MIND'

## SPANISH PROVERB

# CHEESE FONDUE

**DUNCAN MAGUIRE**

## SERVES 6

Equal portions of Beaufort, Comté and Emmental cheese, allow 250g in total per person
1 level teaspoon cornflour
75ml kirsch (cherry brandy)
1 garlic clove, peeled and crushed
⅔ bottle good Savoie white wine, such as Apremont
A good pinch of white pepper
Plenty of slightly stale white baguette, cut into bite-sized cubes, served in a basket

Remove any rind from the cheeses. Grate the cheese finely in the French style of thin strands. In a separate bowl, carefully beat the cornflour into the kirsch, making sure there are no lumps.

In either a fondue pot or heavy-based pan, very slowly melt the cheese with the garlic and the wine, stirring continuously so that it does not burn. When the cheese mixture is smooth, stir in the blended kirsch and cornflour a little at a time, until the cheese mixture thickens. Season with the white pepper and serve bubbling hot with the crusty bread.

# RABBIT BALLOTINE

## DAVE BONE

### SERVES 4

4 slices good-quality Parma ham
4 rabbit loins, butterflied (ask your butcher to do this for you)
A few cavolo nero leaves
1 garlic clove, peeled and finely chopped
1 head of chicory (endive), leaves snapped apart and washed
Mixed salad leaves (experiment with different cresses and salad leaves), washed
1 pomegranate, seeds only (cut into quarters and scrape out the seeds)
A squeeze of lemon
Good-quality olive oil
Salt and pepper

Lay out a large sheet of cling film on a chopping board. Arrange the Parma ham slices in a row along the middle of the cling film, sightly overlapping. Place the rabbit loins over the Parma ham, again slightly overlapping.

Blanch the cavolo nero in boiling water and toss in the garlic and a lug of oil. Drain off the excess water and lay the cavolo nero in a row across the middle of the rabbit. Season with salt and pepper.

Using the cling film, roll the Parma ham, rabbit and cavolo into a log shape and tighten at each end by twisting the cling film so that it looks like a sausage. Tie each end tightly with string and put the ballotine (the sausage) in a pan of cold water, and bring to the boil. When it reaches boiling point, remove the pan from the heat and leave to cool in the water. Once cooled, take the ballotine out of the water and carefully unwrap the cling film.

Lightly toss the chicory and salad leaves and pomegranate seeds with some olive oil and a squeeze of lemon. In a hot frying pan, sear the outside of the ballotine evenly by slowly rolling it in the pan. Then slice it into discs, arrange on the plate with the salad, and enjoy!

# WHITEFISH ROE MOUSSE BLINIS

## RISTO MIKKOLA

### SERVES 8

200ml sour cream
200g white fish roe
30g small red onion, diced
1 tablespoon chopped dill
A pinch of ground black
pepper
Dill sprigs to garnish

### BLINIS

1.25 litres milk
500g buckwheat flour
250g plain flour
15g yeast
1 teaspoon salt
2 eggs, separated
800ml cream
100ml melted butter
Oil for frying

In a mixing bowl, whisk the sour cream until stiff, then add the white fish roe, onion, dill and pepper, and let stand for 1 hour until needed.

### FOR THE BLINIS

Pour 750ml of the milk into a saucepan and warm. Remove from the heat and in a large bowl, mix thoroughly with the buckwheat and plain flours, yeast and salt to form a dough (it will look like a thick batter). Place a tea towel over the mixing bowl and let the dough rest for at least 3 hours.

Heat the remaining milk in a saucepan. Add to the dough in the mixing bowl with the egg yolks, cream and melted butter, and mix thoroughly. In a separate bowl, whisk the egg whites until they form soft peaks, and fold into the dough.

Heat a frying pan until hot, then add a little oil and ladle in a small amount of the batter. Cook for 3 minutes, flip the blinis and cook for a further 3 minutes. The blinis should look like small pancakes, about 8cm across. Remove from the pan and repeat until you have 16 blinis. Reserve until serving.

### TO SERVE

Spoon the fish roe mousse onto the blinis, garnish with sprigs of dill, and serve. For extra flair, you could also add whitefish roe or golden caviar and a little diced shallot.

# MUSSELS COOKED IN BEER WITH CHILLI JAM

## ANT POWER

This could be one of the easiest dishes to cook for a group of hungry Mo Bros and Mo Sistas. The chilli jam makes a great freezer standby when you want to spice up a dish – it goes with curries, stir-fries and just about anything. So freeze any leftover chilli jam in an ice cube tray and you'll be packing some serious heat whenever the need arises. Although before you go nuts adding it to dishes, it's a good idea to try a little of the jam to test the heat – you don't want to destroy your mates' tastebuds.

### SERVES 6

### CHILLI JAM

25ml olive oil
1 Spanish onion, peeled and diced
2 red peppers, deseeded and diced
4 garlic cloves, peeled
3 red chillies
200g cherry tomatoes
50g brown sugar
100ml fish sauce

### MUSSELS

1 bottle of lager
2kg fresh mussels, cleaned
200ml coconut cream
A bunch of fresh coriander, roughly chopped
2 limes, cut into quarters
Oil for cooking

### FOR THE CHILLI JAM

Heat the olive oil in a wok or large saucepan and sauté the onion and red peppers until they are quite dark in colour. Add the whole garlic and chillies and sauté for a further 10 minutes. Add the cherry tomatoes and cook for another 5 minutes. Add the sugar and fish sauce, lower the temperature and cook for 10 minutes.

Remove from the heat, transfer to a blender and blitz to a smooth purée – refrigerate until needed (see above).

### FOR THE MUSSELS

Heat a little oil in a wok or large saucepan until smoking hot. Add 125g of the chilli jam and cook for a few minutes to release all the aromas and flavour.

Pour the lager into the wok and and bring to the boil. Add the mussels, stir and cover with a lid – this will steam the mussels. After a few minutes check the mussels – they should have all opened. Add the coconut cream, stir and bring to the boil.

Sprinkle the coriander over the top and serve in the wok in the middle of the table. Remember the side bowls, lime wedges and lots of napkins.

# PIGEON TERRINE

## WOLFE CONYNGHAM

### SERVES 10

8–10 pigeon breast fillets (ask your butcher for these)
500g pork sausage meat
4 sprigs of thyme, leaves picked
A pinch of salt and a few grinds of black pepper
75ml port
30g unsalted butter
6–8 slices prosciutto
Spring onions, finely chopped (optional)

'THIS ISN'T THE GUN I USED TO SHOOT THESE PIGEONS – I USED A BIGGER ONE'

**WOLFE CONYNGHAM**

Preheat the oven to 160°C/gas mark 3. Roughly chop the pigeon breasts into small chunks and put in a blender. Add the sausage meat, thyme and salt and pepper, and blend to a smooth consistency. Transfer to a large mixing bowl.

In a hot frying pan, add the port and burn off the alcohol by lighting it with a match – be careful not to burn yourself or set fire to the kitchen. Next, add the butter to the pan and melt, and add to the mixing bowl containing the pigeon mixture. Using a spatula, gently fold all the ingredients together.

Line a 1kg loaf tin with the prosciutto slices, ensuring that the entire surface is covered and a little hangs over the edges (this will fold over the top of the terrine once the tin is filled).

Gently pour all the mixture into the loaf tin – it should fill almost to the top. Fold over the excess prosciutto and, to give it a rustic feel, add on top a thin layer of finely chopped spring onions.

Cover the loaf tin with tin foil and place in a baking tray deep enough to allow you to pour in boiling water two-thirds of the way up the sides of the loaf tin. (This bain marie method of cooking allows the heat of the oven to permeate through the water and cook the terrine evenly and very gently.)

Place the tin in the oven and cook for 1–1½ hours or until a skewer inserted comes out piping hot. Once cooked, remove the loaf tin from the baking tray, pour out any excess liquid from the tin and then leave it to cool for 30 minutes at room temperature. Refrigerate overnight.

### TO SERVE

Remove the terrine from the loaf tin by placing an upturned chopping board on the tin and flipping the tin over. Gently tap the bottom and sides of the loaf tin and the terrine should drop out onto the chopping board. Slice the terrine and serve with toasted bread and a nice glass of wine.

# ASPARAGUS, SOFT DUCK EGG, CRISPY HAM AND SHAVED PARMESAN

### DEON JANSEN

### SERVES 6

6 duck eggs
100g thinly sliced Parma ham
2 bunches of asparagus
100g Parmesan shavings
Extra-virgin olive oil for drizzling
Salt

Place the duck eggs in a pan of boiling water and cook for 7 minutes exactly. Transfer to a bowl of iced water to stop them cooking further. When cool, gently peel off the shells and set aside.

Preheat the grill to a medium heat, then grill the Parma ham for 5 minutes or until crispy. Blanch the asparagus in a pan of boiling salted water for 1 minute. Remove and drain.

### TO SERVE

Place the asparagus on the plates. Cut the eggs in half and put 2 halves on each plate. Add the crispy Parma ham and Parmesan shavings, then drizzle with olive oil.

'BACON AND EGGS: A DAY'S
WORK FOR A HEN;
A LIFETIME COMMITMENT
FOR A PIG'

FACT

# LETTUCE WRAPS WITH PHEASANT, ELDERBERRY YOGURT AND FRIED ONIONS

**GILES CLARK**

## SERVES 6

5 shallots
2 pickled onions
500g yogurt
3 pheasants
2 round lettuces, leaves picked and washed
Oil
Salt and pepper
1 onion, peeled, finely sliced and fried until crispy to serve

## ELDERBERRY VINEGAR

50g sugar
100g elderberries
150ml red wine

To make sweet elderberry vinegar, put the sugar, elderberries and red wine in a saucepan and simmer for 40 minutes, skimming off any scum. When cool, press through muslin or a clean damp tea towel. Pour into a sterilised bottle and keep in the fridge for whenever you need it.

Heat some oil in a frying pan. Peel and thinly slice the shallots, and fry in the oil until light golden brown. Remove from the oil and drain on kitchen paper. Season with salt and set aside until serving.

Dice the pickled onions finely and mix through the yogurt along with 80ml of the elderberry vinegar. Season with a little salt.

Preheat the oven to 180°C/gas mark 4. Season the pheasants inside and out with salt and pepper and put in a roasting tray. Roast in the oven for 30 minutes, then remove and set aside for 15 minutes to rest. When they are properly rested, tear all the meat from the bones, including the crispy skin, and put in a bowl. Toss with just enough oil to coat the meat and season with salt.

### TO SERVE

Serve everything in separate dishes on the table so that people can arm themselves with a lettuce leaf, a heap of pheasant meat, a dollop of yogurt and a few fried onions – get stuck in.

# 'REAL' BREAD DOUGH FOCACCIA

**RICHARD ROBINSON**

Britain was once a nation of bakers. Sadly this tradition is lost and most Mo Bros are happy to eat flavourless supermarket bread, mass-produced in huge factories without love and pride, containing preservatives and processed ingredients that are bad for you. This simple bread dough recipe provides dough for focaccia, which will keep for a few days and go perfectly with any of the recipes in this book, as well as for pizza bases (see page 68 for pizza recipes). Surprise your Mo Bros and Mo Sistas by whipping up a heap of homemade pizzas for your next impromptu dinner party instead of ordering take-away.

## BREAD DOUGH

### MAKES 6 PIZZA BASES AND 1 LARGE FOCACCIA LOAF

1kg 'No.4 Shipton Mill' bread
flour or other organic bread
flour
40g semolina
20g fresh yeast
20g sea salt flakes
100ml extra-virgin olive oil

### FOCACCIA

20ml extra-virgin olive oil
10g sea salt flakes
20g rosemary, picked

### FOR THE BREAD DOUGH

In a mixing bowl, combine the bread flour and semolina. Rub in the yeast, using your fingertips as if making a crumble. Form a well and add the salt, olive oil and 640ml warm water. Mix the ingredients, using your hands to bring the dry ingredients up into the wet liquids. Once combined, lift the dough onto a clean work surface. Do not flour or oil the surface – the dough may look sticky, but it will all come together after kneading. Knead the dough by squashing it with the ball of your hand, then push it away from you to stretch it, pull it back to a ball, give it a quarter turn and repeat. Do this for 10–15 minutes.

Transfer the dough to a floured bowl and leave to rise for an hour in a warm place, until it has roughly doubled in size. Once risen, turn the dough out and divide into two equal portions – one for focaccia bread and one for pizza bases.

### FOR THE FOCACCIA

Place the focaccia dough portion on an oiled baking tray and spread the dough out so it covers the tray and is about 2.5cm thick. Cover with a tea towel and allow to rise again for 1 hour.

Once risen, preheat the oven to 200C/gas mark 6. Prod the dough with your fingers to create dimples and drizzle with a little extra olive oil. Sprinkle on the sea salt and rosemary and cook in the oven for 15–20 minutes until golden brown. Remove from the oven and cool on a wire rack. Brush with a little more olive oil while still hot and serve with any of the dishes in this book or with small bowls of quality extra-virgin olive oil and balsamic vinegar.

# 'REAL' BREAD DOUGH PIZZA

**RICHARD ROBINSON**

## SERVES 6

Dough for pizza bases (see recipe on previous page)

## TOMATO SAUCE BASE

100g shallots, peeled and chopped
2 garlic cloves, peeled and sliced
2 tablespoons olive oil
500g perfectly ripe tomatoes, halved
200ml chicken stock
1 sprig of thyme
1 sprig of rosemary
Salt and black pepper

## SUGGESTED PIZZA TOPPINGS

- Buffalo mozzarella, tomato and basil
- Mushrooms, ricotta, spinach and egg
- Anchovies, tomato, mozzarella, capers and olives
- Goat's cheese, tomatoes, onion and pesto
- Salami, tomato, mozzarella and chilli flakes
- Squirrel, spinach and pine nuts
- Spicy sausage, mozzarella and broccoli

## FOR THE TOMATO SAUCE BASE

In a heavy-based pan, sweat the shallots and garlic in the olive oil until golden brown. Add the tomatoes and chicken stock and, on a low heat, reduce for 30 minutes until the tomatoes have collapsed and the liquid has almost gone. Transfer to a blender and blitz until smooth. (You can make this well in advance and it also freezes well.)

## FOR THE PIZZAS

Preheat the oven to 240°C/gas mark 9 or the hottest setting your oven will reach. For the pizza base, divide the dough into 6 balls. Gently flatten one dough ball, pushing out from the centre into the shape you want. Don't worry if your pizza base is not perfect; simply tell your guests you are going for the 'rustic' look.

Transfer the pizza base to an oiled baking tray or oven stone. Spread on your tomato sauce and top with just about anything you fancy. Repeat with the remaining dough balls. Place the pizza in the oven and cook for 10–15 minutes. (If you want to make only 1 pizza base, wrap each dough ball in cling film and freeze until needed.)

# COOK
# BARBECUES

# BARBECUED PORK CHOPS WITH WARM ROAST PUMPKIN, BEETROOT, SPINACH, LENTIL AND RED PEPPER SALAD

## ANT POWER

### SERVES 6

1 large butternut squash, peeled, deseeded and diced into 2.5cm cubes
200g sunflower seeds
200g pumpkin seeds
250g Puy lentils
6 red peppers
6 medium cooked beetroot, peeled and diced
500g baby spinach, roughly chopped
50ml balsamic vinegar
100ml extra-virgin olive oil, plus extra for cooking
100g feta cheese
6 pork loin chops
Salt and pepper

### TARRAGON AND MUSTARD MAYO

200g light mayonnaise
A bunch of tarragon, finely chopped
100g capers, drained
20g Dijon mustard
10g English mustard
½ bunch of parsley, picked and finely chopped
A squeeze of lemon juice

Mix together all the mayonnaise ingredients in a bowl. (This can be prepared the day before.)

Preheat the oven to 200°C/gas mark 6. Toss the diced squash with a little olive oil and roast for about 30 minutes until caramelised and softened. At the same time place the sunflower and pumpkin seeds on a baking tray and toast in the oven for about 10 minutes. Set aside.

Put the lentils in a saucepan with 3 cups of water and a pinch of salt. Bring to the boil, reduce the heat and simmer for about 15 minutes or until cooked. Drain and set aside.

Light the barbecue and appreciate man's ability to make fire – especially with the aid of firelighters. Place the red peppers on the barbecue and cook until they turn black. Remove from the flames, place in a bowl, cover with cling film and steam for 10 minutes (this will allow the skin to peel away from the flesh). Under running water, peel off the blackened, blistered skin – don't be too fussy as the burnt bits will have a rich smoky flavour. Then halve and deseed the peppers and set aside.

In a large serving dish, add the beetroot and spinach. Mix together the vinegar and 100ml olive oil and toss through the salad. Crumble the feta over the top and set aside while you cook the pork chops.

When the barbecue is hot, lightly oil the pork and season well with salt and pepper. Cook until just cooked through – about 5 minutes each side; be careful not to overcook as they will be tough and as dry as your moustache.

### TO SERVE

Place a pork chop on each plate and a generous spoonful of salad. Put the mayonnaise nearby for all to share.

# BARBECUED RUMP OF BEEF, BEETROOT AND FETA AND POTATO SALAD

### MARC AND CONOR BEREEN

## SERVES 6

### BEEF

2kg rump of beef
Olive oil
Fresh ground black pepper

### BEETROOT AND FETA SALAD

100g walnuts
5 bunches of baby beetroot
200g feta cheese
Extra-virgin olive oil
Salt and pepper

### POTATO SALAD

20 baby potatoes, washed (skin on)
100g cornichons, roughly chopped
50g capers, drained
100g mayonnaise
Salt and pepper

### FOR THE BEEF

Marinate the beef by rubbing over 2 tablespoons olive oil and seasoning generously with fresh ground black pepper. Put on a plate, cover with cling film and leave out of the fridge for 2 hours before cooking.

Heat the barbecue. Salt the beef generously and seal on the grill, fat-side down, at a medium temperature for about 10 minutes or until nicely charred. Seal on the other side for a further 5 minutes. Turn down the heat to its lowest level and cook for a further 45 minutes, turning occasionally to prevent burning. The meat should be medium rare at this stage (invest in a meat thermometer and you won't need to guess). Remove from the barbecue and rest the meat for 30 minutes before carving.

### FOR THE BEETROOT AND FETA SALAD

In a frying pan, lightly toast the walnuts. Then cool. In a saucepan, boil the beetroot for 25 minutes. Then cool and peel the skin off – it should fall off to reveal ripe, purple baby beetroot. Cut the beetroots in half and place in a mixing bowl. Crumble the feta and toss together with the beetroots, walnuts and a little extra-virgin olive oil. Season to taste with salt and pepper.

### FOR THE POTATO SALAD

In a large saucepan, cover the potatoes with cold water and bring to the boil. Turn down the heat and simmer until cooked. (A knife should easily cut through one when cooked.) Drain and allow to cool. When cooled, cut the potatoes into quarters, place in a bowl with the cornichons, capers and mayonnaise and toss together. Season to taste.

### TO SERVE

Carve the rested meat and serve in a large dish along with the potato salad and beetroot salad.

'WITH A GREAT MOUSTACHE COMES GREAT RESPONSIBILITY'
PETER GRIFFIN, *FAMILY GUY*

# BARBECUED CHERMOULA CHICKEN, TABBOULEH, GOOD TIMES

## ANT POWER

As you baste your chicken with the chermoula marinade, you could explain to your guests that chermoula is an ancient recipe from Tunisia and Algeria. Many moons ago, when it was more highly prized than gold, rival kings fought over whose recipe was superior and who could rightfully lay claim to the title 'The Sultan of Sizzle'.

## SERVES 8

### CHERMOULA MARINADE

A bunch of parsley, picked
A bunch of coriander with the stems on, washed
A bunch of spring onions, chopped
3 garlic cloves, peeled and chopped
2 tablespoons Spanish smoked paprika
2 tablespoons ground cumin
2 tablespoons sumac (a purple spicy berry)
4 tablespoons ground coriander
1 tablespoon chilli powder
50ml lemon juice
150ml olive oil
Salt and pepper to taste

### TABBOULEH

500g bulgur wheat (available at any good supermarket)
75ml lemon juice
100ml olive oil
A bunch of mint, finely chopped
A bunch of parsley, finely chopped
1 cucumber, seeds removed and diced
3 tomatoes, skin on, deseeded and diced
Salt and pepper

### CHICKEN

8 man-sized chicken breast fillets, skin on (you could also use chicken wings)

## FOR THE CHERMOULA MARINADE

Place all the ingredients in a blender and blitz. Make this the day before your barbecue. If possible, marinate the chicken with a generous amount of the chermoula overnight in the fridge, but make sure you reserve some chermoula for basting the chicken while it cooks.

## FOR THE TABBOULEH

Place the bulgur wheat in a bowl, pour over the lemon juice, olive oil and 500ml boiling water and cover with cling film. Leave for 5–10 minutes to allow the wheat to cook and absorb the liquid. Remove the cling film and fluff with a fork. Allow to cool completely.

Put the bulgur wheat, chopped herbs and vegetables in a large salad bowl and mix. Season with a little salt and pepper. Set aside.

## FOR THE CHICKEN

Heat the barbecue until it's hot, then cook the chicken for 20–25 minutes until its juices run clear, whilst dazzling your guests with random, improbable drivel (see introduction to recipe).

## TO SERVE

Announce to the party that the chermoula chicken is ready and ask each guest to arm themselves with a plate, help themselves to the tabbouleh, and form a line to the barbie where they shall receive their sustenance.

Best enjoyed with sun, ice-cold beer and reggae music.

# RESPECT FOR ANOTHER MAN'S BARBECUE

As the Gentleman's Code instructs: when attending a barbecue at another man's house, a gentleman shall never, under any circumstances, take the liberty of adjusting, turning, prodding, flipping or interfering with the meats cooking on the grill. This is considered an insult to the host of the highest degree and is punishable by flogging in some countries. Furthermore – despite personal cooking preferences – a man should never tell the host when he believes the meats are cooked.

There is of course an international understanding that while men should not touch another's barbecue, they are invited to gather in a tight semi-circle around the barbecue, beer in hand, offering unsolicited advice on matters of temperature, effective lighting techniques and optimum coal distribution. This ritualistic behaviour is often punctuated with long periods of silence as the men stare blankly, hypnotised by the marvel of fire.

# GRILLED CORNISH SQUID SALAD, CHILLI AND GRAPE GREMOLATA

**SAM WILSON**

## SERVES 8

### SQUID SALAD

700g squid, cleaned (you can
ask your fishmonger to do this)
4 small heads of red chicory
(endive), cut into quarters
100g watercress, picked
Oil for grilling
Salt and pepper

### GREMOLATA

A small bunch of red grapes,
cut into quarters
A bunch of of parsley, finely
chopped
Juice and zest of 1 lemon
1 garlic clove, finely chopped
1 red chilli, julienned (cut into
thin strips)
70ml olive oil
Salt and pepper

Heat the barbecue. Score the squid by running your knife gently through the flesh on an angle at 0.5cm spaces in a crisscross fashion, being careful not to cut all the way through. This makes the squid curl up when cooked and adds extra smoky flavour. Keep the tentacles whole.

Lightly oil and grill the red chicory on the barbecue to add smoky flavour. Remove and leave to cool at room temperature. While the chicory cools, mix all the gremolata ingredients in a bowl.

Season the squid with salt and pepper and grill on the barbecue for a few minutes until cooked. Transfer to a chopping board and cut the squid into smaller pieces.

### TO SERVE

Mix the chicory and watercress together in a large bowl. Divide evenly between the plates. Place the squid on top, drizzle with the gremolata and serve immediately.

'WHEN ONE HAS TASTED IT
[WATERMELON] HE KNOWS
WHAT THE ANGELS EAT'

MARK TWAIN

# BARBECUED CHILLI SQUID, THAI BASIL WATERMELON SALAD, CHILLI CARAMEL

**DEON JANSEN**

## SERVES 4

### SQUID

1kg prepared squid and tentacles (the fishmonger will do this for you), body cut into strips
Salt and pepper
A drizzle of oil

### CHILLI CARAMEL

300g palm sugar
A pinch of dried chilli flakes
1 fresh chilli, deseeded and diced
Juice of 1 lime

### WATERMELON SALAD

1 watermelon
A bunch of Thai basil, leaves picked (available from Asian grocery stores)
A bunch of coriander, leaves picked
1 red chilli, deseeded and julienned (sliced into fine strips – watch those fingers!)
2 tablespoons sesame seeds
A bunch of spring onions, sliced on an angle
3 tablespoons fish sauce (this stuff stinks but tastes like heaven when used correctly)
Juice of 1 lime
1 tablespoon sugar

## FOR THE SQUID

Heat up the barbie till she's hot! Salt and pepper those bad boys (the squid), drizzle some oil on the barbecue, then grill. The squid will take only a minute or two to cook.

## FOR THE CHILLI CARAMEL

Place all the ingredients in a pan, add 30ml water, and gently heat until all the sugar has dissolved. Bring to a simmer and bubble until golden brown with a texture like sun. Remove from the heat and cool. This will make enough for 10 portions and it will keep for two weeks.

## FOR THE WATERMELON SALAD

Peel the watermelon, remove as many seeds as possible, then dice. Place all the salad ingredients in a large bowl and toss everything together with a pinch of love.

## TO SERVE

Place the barbecued squid on top of the salad, drizzle with the chilli caramel and enjoy!

# BARBECUED PRAWNS WITH PIRI PIRI

## MARC AND CONOR BEREEN

### SERVES 6

4 red chillies, finely diced and deseeded
2 shallots, peeled and finely diced
3 garlic cloves, peeled and finely diced
Olive oil
1kg whole prawns

In a saucepan, place the chillies, shallots and garlic and enough olive oil to cover, and simmer for 5 minutes. Remove from the heat and cool. When cooled completely, mix in with the prawns and marinate for 4 hours in the fridge.

Heat the barbecue. Toss the marinated prawns evenly over the flames and cook for just over a minute each side. Transfer to a serving dish and drizzle on a little more piri piri for added kick. Don't forget the napkins.

# DAVIS FAMILY PORK RIBS

**OISIN DAVIS**

The following recipe is a culmination of the efforts of three of my stateside uncles, hence the name Davis Family Pork Ribs. The dry spice mix is my Uncle Brian's. He taught me the recipe many moons ago when I spent a night in his house during a Christmas break. When he learned that my favourite food was 'anything barbecued', he splashed out on a brand-new barbecue and we had a cookout in his garden during a severe Pennsylvania snowstorm. A few years later, on a hot New Jersey summer evening, my Uncle Eddie showed me how to make his famous thick, gooey, sweet and spicy basting sauce. Armed with these two nuggets of gold, it was my Uncle Jimmy who completed the circle and shared with me the secret to cooking perfectly tender ribs where the meat literally falls off the bone. The secret, he told me: cook them overnight in the oven wrapped in cling film. Ribs cooked to this recipe would be my choice for my last meal in this life.

## SERVES 6

2 whole racks of baby back
pork ribs

## BASTING SAUCE

2 tablespoons olive oil
1 large onion, peeled and
chopped
3 garlic cloves, peeled and
crushed
1 tablespoon ground chilli
125ml red wine or cider
vinegar
2 tablespoons fresh lime juice
600ml tomato passata
100ml molasses or 100g
molasses sugar
2 teaspoons mustard powder
2 bay leaves
½ teaspoon salt

## DRY SPICE MIX

1 tablespoon dark brown sugar
2 tablespoons paprika
1 tablespoon mild chilli powder
1 tablespoon ground
black pepper
1 teaspoon cayenne pepper
2 tablespoons salt

## FOR THE BASTING SAUCE

In a medium-sized saucepan, add the olive oil and heat over a high heat. Add the onions and cook for 4–5 minutes until they are slightly browned. Add the garlic and chilli, and cook for a further minute. Deglaze the pan with the vinegar and lime juice and cook until the liquid is reduced by half. Add the tomato passata, molasses, mustard, bay leaves and salt. Bring to a simmer and cook for 15–20 minutes, stirring occasionally, until thick. Remove from the heat and strain. Set aside.

## FOR THE PORK RIBS

Preheat the oven to 110°C/gas mark ¼ or as low as it will go. Combine all the dry spice mix ingredients and then rub on the pork ribs so they're well covered. Wrap a few layers of good-quality cling film around the ribs, keeping them as airtight as possible, and put them in the oven – don't worry, the cling film won't melt! (Check the label to see if it's safe for use in the oven, and if not, use tin foil instead.) Leave the ribs in the oven for as long as you can – a minimum of 6 hours at this temperature is required. A good idea is to place them in the oven when you go to bed and take them out 8 hours later when you wake.

Remove the ribs from the oven and try to resist eating them for breakfast unless you log trees or ride bulls for a living. When cooled, remove the cling film and let the ribs rest for as long as you can resist and then baste with the sauce. Grill them on your barbecue or stick them under your grill in the kitchen. Give them another basting with the sauce before you finish grilling them.

## TO SERVE

Serve with just about anything you wish, such as baked potatoes, coleslaw, salad and buckets of ice-cold beers. If you have Mo Sistas joining your Movember cook-up, you might want to have some finger bowls of water and lemon slices so they can wash their sauce-stained fingers.

COOK
MEAT

# ROAST PORK BELLY STIR-FRY WITH ROAST CHILLI PASTE

**BRAD STOWARD**

The first thing to remember when trying to catch a pig is to look inconspicuous. Fine tweed and cricket sweaters will fool even the wiliest piglet into thinking you are a gentleman and their friend. Casual conversation or comment on the topic of moustaches will further strengthen this belief and relax them, allowing you to assess the more succulent belly. This belly takes a few hours to prepare and is then stir-fried in a Thai roasted chilli paste.

## SERVES 6

750g pork belly
6 teaspoons white vinegar
3 teaspoons salt
Vegetable oil for deep-frying

### ROAST CHILLI PASTE

9 red shallots, peeled
6 garlic cloves, peeled
10–15 dried red chillies
Banana leaf (available from Asian grocers) or tin foil
A pinch of salt
20g palm sugar
Groundnut oil

### TO FINISH

240g green beans
30g fresh large red chillies, sliced
15g Thai basil (available from Asian grocers)
Banana leaves
Oil for cooking

## FOR THE PORK BELLY

Blanch the pork belly in simmering, salted water until it is tender to the touch but slightly springy; this should take about 15 minutes. Drain and hang in a cool place for about 2–3 hours, or until dry. When dry, cut into 3cm strips along the length of the pork belly. This will make it easier to fry skin-side down.

Mix the vinegar and salt and rub into the flesh of the pork. Allow to dry on a wire rack for a further 3 hours.

Pour oil into a heavy-based pan or wok until two-thirds full, then heat the oil over a medium heat until it's around 180°C. (If you don't have a thermometer, drop a 3cm cube of bread into the oil and if it turns golden and crispy the oil should be at the right temperature.) Deep-fry the pork skin-side down until it begins to crackle and bubble. Be very careful as the skin will burn if you come into contact with it. Remove the pork belly from the oil and drain on a wire rack. Allow to cool and then slice into bite-sized pieces.

## FOR THE ROAST CHILLI PASTE

Wrap the shallots, garlic and dried chillies in a banana leaf or tin foil and grill under a low heat for 15 minutes. Remove the roasted ingredients from the banana leaf or foil, place in a pestle and mortar and pound to form a coarse paste. Season with the salt and sugar, and moisten with a little oil. The sauce should taste hot and salty.

## TO FINISH

Heat a little oil in a wok or heavy-based pan and add the chilli paste. Cook for a couple of minutes, stirring constantly to release the flavours. Add the pork belly pieces and stir. Add the green beans and cook for a couple of minutes. If it's a little dry, add a dash of water. Finally, add the fresh chilli and Thai basil. Remove from the heat and serve on banana leaves if you have them.

# ARROZ AL HORNO WITH FRESH TOMATO SAUCE

**SIMON FERNANDEZ**

This is a traditional oven-baked rice dish from Valencia in Spain with pork ribs, chipolata sausages, lots of garlic, sliced potatoes, tomatoes, beans and asparagus.

## SERVES 8

7 chicken stock cubes
750g potatoes, peeled and thinly sliced
24 chipolata sausages
16 pork ribs
14 garlic cloves, peeled
2 tablespoons cumin seeds
5 chillies, deseeded
3 large mushrooms, washed and sliced

9 capiscum (long, thin green peppers), chopped into rings
100ml white wine
500g Arborio rice
400g ripe cherry plum tomatoes
400g green beans, trimmed
2 bunches of asparagus, trimmed
Extra-virgin olive oil for cooking
Salt and pepper

## TOMATO SAUCE

100ml extra-virgin olive oil
200g onions, peeled and chopped
8 plum tomatoes, chopped
1 garlic clove, peeled and crushed
1 chicken stock cube
½ teaspoon rock salt
250ml white wine
5ml white wine vinegar
10 basil leaves

## FOR THE TOMATO SAUCE

In a heavy-based saucepan, heat the oil, add the onions and cook without colouring until soft. Add the tomatoes, mix well and cook for 5 minutes on a medium heat. Add the garlic, chicken stock cube and salt, and cook until the tomatoes are soft. Add the white wine and vinegar, reduce the heat and simmer gently for 20 minutes.

Blitz with a hand blender, pass through a sieve and set aside until serving.

## FOR THE BAKED RICE

Preheat the oven to 200°C/gas mark 6. Dissolve the stock cubes in 2.25 litres water and put to one side. Place the sliced potatoes on an oiled shallow roasting tray, coat in olive oil, season with salt and pepper, and cook in the oven for 6 minutes. Turn the potatoes over and cook for a further 6 minutes.

Once the potatoes are golden brown, take them out of the oven, remove from the roasting tray and put to one side. Add a touch more oil to the roasting tray and return it to the oven to keep the oil sizzling hot. Turn the oven down to 190°C/gas mark 5.

In a large frying pan, cook the sausages, pork ribs, garlic and cumin in a little oil for about 5 minutes until they start to brown (you will need to do this in batches). Remove from the heat and transfer the sausages and ribs to a plate, discarding the garlic cloves. Put a little more oil in the frying pan and over a gentle heat fry the chillies, mushrooms, capiscum and white wine for about 10 minutes or until soft.

Remove the roasting tray from the oven and add the sausages, pork ribs and contents from both saucepans; they should sizzle as they hit the oil. Pour the rice evenly into the roasting tray, add the reserved stock and stir through. Layer the potato slices on top and then add a top layer of tomatoes. Bake for 15 minutes, then reduce the temperature to its lowest setting and bake for an additional 10 minutes. At this point, the rice should be cooked through – check it and return to the oven for an extra 5–10 minutes if not.

## TO SERVE

Bring a pan of salted water to the boil and blanch the beans and asparagus for 3 minutes. Drain and divide them between the plates along with the baked rice. Tear the basil leaves and stir through the tomato sauce and spoon over the rice. Serve immediately.

# THAI LON OF PORK AND PRAWN WITH GRILLED SEA BASS

**BRAD STOWARD**

## SERVES 6

2 tablespoons groundnut oil
2 shallots, peeled and sliced
10g garlic, finely chopped
30g fresh ginger, finely sliced
1 stalk of lemongrass, finely sliced
30g chilli, finely sliced
75g pork mince
100ml coconut milk
3 whole or 6 fillets sea bass
200g tiger prawns
30ml fish sauce
30g sugar
Juice of 1 lime
Coriander and mint for garnish

In a deep pan, add the oil and gently fry the shallots until golden. Add the garlic, ginger, lemongrass and chilli and sauté for 2 minutes. Add the pork mince and break it up so you don't have big lumps. When the pork has browned, add the coconut milk and bring to the boil.

Heat a griddle pan over a high heat, lightly oil the sea bass, place it in the pan and season. After about 4 minutes you should be able to turn the sea bass without it breaking; if it still sticks to the pan, it needs more time to cook.

Meanwhile, add the prawns, fish sauce and sugar to the pan containing the pork. Taste for correct seasoning; it should be sweet, salty and sour.

## TO SERVE

When the prawns are cooked (after about 3 minutes), remove the mixture from the heat, add the lime juice and place in serving bowls. Garnish with fresh coriander and mint leaves. When the sea bass is cooked, serve alongside the prawn lon.

# LAMB, POMEGRANATE COUSCOUS AND SUMAC LABNA

## ANT POWER

This Moroccan-influenced dish has fresh, light flavours that go perfectly with lamb, although it also works well with chicken or salmon. Sumac labna, a strained yogurt flavoured with the tangy, lemony Sumac berry, needs to be left overnight in the fridge to thicken up.

### SERVES 2

1 rack of lamb, French trimmed
Salt and pepper
Olive oil

### SUMAC LABNA

200g natural Greek yogurt
2 tablespoons ground sumac

### COUSCOUS

200ml vegetable stock or water
A pinch of saffron threads (optional)
60ml extra-virgin olive oil
200g couscous
1 fresh pomegranate, seeds only (cut into quarters and scrape out seeds)
1 small red onion, peeled and finely diced
A handful of chopped coriander
A handful of chopped mint
A handful of chopped parsley
50g toasted almond flakes (optional)
Salt and pepper
Juice of 1 lemon

### FOR THE SUMAC LABNA

Line a sieve with a piece of muslin or a clean tea towel and sit over a bowl. Empty the yogurt into the sieve, cover the top with cling film, and leave to strain for about 8 hours in the fridge. Remove the yogurt from the fridge, discard the excess liquid and you are left with a firm, thick yogurt. Mix the sumac into the yogurt.

### FOR THE LAMB

When the sumac labna is ready, preheat the oven to 220°C/gas mark 7. Season the lamb racks with salt and pepper. Heat a little oil in a large ovenproof frying pan and sear the lamb for 2–3 minutes until golden brown. Transfer to the oven and roast for 8 minutes for rare, 10 minutes for medium and 12–15 minutes for well done. Take out of the oven and rest for 10 minutes.

### FOR THE COUSCOUS

In a saucepan, place the vegetable stock and saffron, and bring to the boil. Add half the olive oil. Put the couscous in a bowl, pour the stock over, and cover with cling film. Let it stand for 5 minutes, then, using a fork, separate the couscous. Before serving, mix the remaining ingredients, except the lemon juice, into the couscous. Add the lemon juice at the last minute.

### TO SERVE

Carve the lamb into cutlets and serve with the couscous and sumac labna.

# ELWY VALLEY LAMB AND LIVER WITH ARTICHOKES, BABY BEETS AND WILD MUSHROOMS

RICHARD ROBINSON

## SERVES 6

### BABY BEETS

2 bunches of baby beetroot
80ml olive oil
25ml sherry vinegar
1 garlic clove, peeled and
crushed
1 sprig of thyme
1 bay leaf
Salt

### MUSHROOMS

20g butter
1 shallot, peeled and diced
½ garlic clove, peeled and
finely diced
1 sprig of thyme
300g mixed wild mushrooms
6 baby artichokes (you can get
these from a good delicatessen)
Salt and cracked black pepper

### FENNEL PURÉE

100g unsalted butter
600g fennel, trimmed and sliced
Salt and cracked black pepper
50ml white wine
250ml chicken stock

### LAMB RUMP AND LIVER

4 lamb rumps
Salt and freshly cracked
black pepper
50g unsalted butter
1 lamb liver, cleaned and
thinly sliced (ask your
butcher to do this)
Milk
1 tablespoon olive oil

### FOR THE BABY BEETS

Remove the tops of the beetroots and reserve for a leafy garnish. Wash and boil the beetroots in salted water for 10–15 minutes until tender. When cooked, refresh in cold water and peel the outer skin from the beetroots. Place in a bowl and toss with the oil, sherry vinegar, garlic, thyme and bay leaf, and set aside.

### FOR THE MUSHROOMS

In a heavy-based saucepan, gently melt the butter until it starts to foam. Add the shallot, garlic and thyme, and sweat over a low heat until translucent. Add the mushrooms and artichokes, increase the heat and cook until just soft. Season with salt and pepper and set aside until serving.

### FOR THE FENNEL PURÉE

Heat the butter in a medium saucepan over a low heat until it starts to foam. Then add the sliced fennel and seasoning, place the lid on top and sweat the fennel until it starts to turn transparent. Deglaze the pan with the wine and cook until the liquid is reduced to syrup. Add the stock and cook until the fennel is tender and the stock has cooked right down. Transfer to a blender and purée until smooth. Chill in the fridge.

### FOR THE LAMB RUMP

Preheat the oven to 200°C/gas mark 6. Heat a frying pan until hot. Season the lamb rumps with salt and pepper and sear in the pan with half the butter for 1–2 minutes until browned. Transfer to the preheated oven and cook for 4–6 minutes for rare, 6–8 minutes for medium. Remove from the oven and rest on a cooling rack for about 10 minutes.

### FOR THE LAMB LIVER

Soak the liver in just enough milk to cover them for 20 minutes before cooking. Remove from the milk, pat dry with a paper towel, and season with salt and pepper. In a hot pan, heat the oil and remaining butter, and sauté for about 3 minutes until cooked pink. Remove and rest for a few minutes before serving.

### TO SERVE

If necessary, reheat the mushrooms and fennel purée. Slice the lamb rumps into even-size slices. Smear 2 tablespoons of fennel purée on each plate. Arrange the sliced rump and liver on the plates and spoon over the wild mushrooms and beetroot.

# BEEF BOURGUIGNON, POTATO AND PARSNIP MASH

## LUCA AND GUGLIELMO D'ALFONSO

### SERVES 6

### BOURGUIGNON

50ml extra-virgin olive oil, plus extra for frying
3 garlic cloves, peeled
50g smoked bacon lardons
2 onions, peeled and finely chopped
1 leek, trimmed and finely chopped
4 shallots, peeled and finely chopped
4 carrots, peeled and roughly chopped
4 celery sticks, roughly chopped
A bunch of parsley
100g fresh, good-quality mixed mushrooms, washed and thinly sliced
1kg shin of beef, diced
100g plain flour
Sprigs of thyme or rosemary
1 cinnamon stick
1 bay leaf
2 x 400g cans plum tomatoes
1 bottle Chianti or Barolo
Salt and pepper

### POTATO AND PARSNIP MASH

5 large Rooster potatoes, peeled and roughly chopped
4 parsnips, peeled and roughly chopped
2 red onions, peeled and chopped
The remainder of the red wine
20ml balsamic vinegar
1 teaspoon sugar
50g butter
50g single cream
Salt and pepper
A little grated nutmeg

### FOR THE BOURGUIGNON

In a large ovenproof casserole dish, heat the olive oil. Add 2 of the garlic cloves and the bacon lardons. Cook for 3 minutes on a medium heat, then add the chopped onions, leek, shallots, carrots and celery and cook on a low heat for a further 15 minutes.

Meanwhile, thinly slice the remaining garlic clove and parsley stalks (either discard the leaves or use them as garnish). Put a little olive oil in a frying pan and sweat the garlic and parsley together, taking care not to burn the garlic. After a few minutes, add the mushrooms and cook on a low heat until softened.

Preheat the oven to 180°C/gas mark 4. Lightly coat the diced shin of beef with the plain flour and add to the casserole dish with the thyme or rosemary sprigs, shaking off any excess flour beforehand. When the meat has browned all over (this will take about 5 minutes and you will need to do it in batches), add the cinnamon stick, bay leaf and mushroom mix from the frying pan, the plum tomatoes and 400ml of the red wine. Season with salt and pepper. Bring the dish to the boil and then put on its lid and put in the preheated oven for at least 2½ hours. It is ready when the meat is so tender that it can be easily broken up with a fork. Remove from the oven, check the seasoning and adjust if necessary.

### FOR THE POTATO AND PARSNIP MASH

Place the roughly chopped potato and parsnip in a saucepan and bring to the boil in salted water. Meanwhile, fry the chopped red onion in a dash of olive oil. When softened, add the remainder of the red wine, the balsamic vinegar and the sugar. Simmer until the liquid has reduced and the onions taste sweet.

When the potato and parsnip are cooked, drain them in a colander, letting them steam for a few minutes to release their moisture. Put them back in the saucepan and add the caramelised onions, butter, cream, salt and pepper, then grate in a little nutmeg. Blend everything together with a hand blender. Season to taste.

### TO SERVE

Place the pans with the potato and parsnip mash and Bourguignon on a heatproof mat or board in the middle of the table and serve with crusty bread.

'DON'T GET STRESSED. NO ONE LIKES AN UNHAPPY HOST. A MO BRO IS MEASURED AND IN COMPLETE CONTROL'

# VENISON WITH CHARRED SWEETCORN, MASHED POTATO, ROAST PARSNIPS AND PORT AND REDCURRANT JUS

### ANDY WAUGH AND RUARIDH EMSLIE

## SERVES 6

6 parsnips, peeled and quartered
300g potatoes, peeled and cut into small chunks
50g butter
180g sweetcorn, canned is fine but corn on the cob is better
Roasted mixed seeds, such as pumpkin or sunflower
6 x 150g venison topside or loin steaks
Olive oil
Salt and pepper

## PORT AND REDCURRANT JUS

A knob of butter
4 shallots, peeled and sliced
2 fresh thyme sprigs
2 garlic cloves, peeled and chopped
50g dark brown sugar
400ml red wine
1½ tablespoons good-quality port
30g tomato paste
50g redcurrant jelly

Preheat the oven to 180°C /gas mark 4. Place the parsnips in a shallow roasting dish, toss with a little olive oil and roast in the oven for about 1 hour until golden brown.

Put the chunks of potatoes in a pan of salted water and bring to the boil. Reduce the heat and simmer for 20 minutes until tender. When cooked, drain and mash together with the butter. Once the butter is mashed through, season, then mash further until really smooth.

For the port and redcurrant jus, melt the knob of butter in a large saucepan on a medium-to-high heat. Add the shallots, thyme sprigs and garlic and fry for 2–3 minutes. Stir in the brown sugar until it melts through and begins to bubble up the side of the pan. Reduce the heat, stir in the red wine, port, tomato paste and redcurrant jelly. Bring to the boil and simmer for 15 minutes – this will evaporate off most of the alcohol, leaving a rich, sweet and syrup-like sauce. Remove and discard the thyme sprigs.

Cut the kernels from the cob (or drain if you're using the canned stuff) and place in a dry frying pan on a medium-to-high heat. Cook the kernels until they begin to char and turn golden brown. When nearly done, add the mixed seeds and lightly toast with the corn to release the flavours. Place in a bowl and keep in a warm place.

Put the venison on a plate to allow it to relax and warm to room temperature. Place the same pan that you cooked the corn in on the hob, get it as hot as possible and wipe a very small amount of oil around it. Season the venison with salt and pepper on each side and place in the pan. Reduce the heat a little and cook on each side for 2 minutes for rare or 3½ minutes for medium. Allow the meat to rest in a warm place for 5 minutes.

## TO SERVE

Put a good-size tablespoon of the potato in the middle of each plate. Place 4 or 5 parsnip quarters around the outside. Slice the steak across the grain into 4 or 5 pieces and place on top of the potato. Sprinkle over the sweetcorn and seeds and drizzle with the jus.

# ROAST RABBIT WITH CRISPY WILD MUSHROOM RAVIOLI

**MARC BEREEN AND CIARAN MCGONAGLE**

There are a few methods employed by people around the world to hunt rabbit: traps, ferrets, dynamite and the shotgun. However, a true gentleman prefers to go au naturel and simply reach down into the warren and grab one using his bare hands.

## SERVES 4

### RAVIOLI

275g '00' flour
7 eggs
5 tablespoons olive oil
1 shallot, peeled and diced
2 garlic cloves, peeled and chopped
300g mixed mushrooms, thinly sliced
250g ricotta
2 tablespoons chopped parsley
100g grated pecorino
2 tablespoons milk
Salt and pepper

### RABBIT

4 rabbit legs
100g unsalted butter
1 tablespoon chopped parsley
1 tablespoon chopped tarragon
1 garlic clove, peeled and chopped
Grated rind of 1 lemon
20 thin bacon slices
4 racks of rabbit
Salt and pepper

### TO FINISH AND OPTIONAL GARNISH

1 tablespoon butter
100g girolle mushrooms
8 baby leeks, halved
8 fine asparagus spears, halved
12 cherry tomatoes, halved
Fresh figs, sliced to garnish
A few sprigs of chervil to garnish

### FOR THE RAVIOLI

In a large mixing bowl, place the flour, egg yolks from 4 eggs, 1 egg (white included) and 1 tablespoon of the olive oil. Stir with a wooden spoon to make a stiff dough. On a well-floured surface, knead the dough for 10–15 minutes until smooth and elastic and no longer sticky. Wrap the dough in cling film and rest for 30 minutes.

Heat 2 tablespoons of the olive oil in a heavy-based pan over a medium heat. Add the shallot and garlic and sauté until the garlic just begins to brown. Add the mushrooms and cook for about 10 minutes, or until golden brown. Transfer to a bowl and cool. When cooled, add the ricotta, parsley, pecorino and 1 beaten egg, season with salt and pepper.

Cut the pasta dough in half. On a floured surface, roll out both halves of the dough very thinly, about 3mm thick. Drop tablespoons of filling (enough to make around 4 large ravioli circles) 2–3cm apart, on one sheet of the pasta. Mix 1 beaten egg with the milk and then brush onto the other sheet of pasta. Place the second sheet of pasta, egg side-down, on top of the first sheet. Gently press around each filling to seal. Using a ravioli cutter or sharp knife, cut a circle around each filling mound, leaving a 1cm border. Allow to rest for 10 minutes.

### FOR THE RABBIT

Preheat the oven to 220°C/gas mark 7. With a small, sharp knife, remove the thigh bone from each rabbit leg, by forming a little tunnel around the bone, rather than cutting through the side. This is a little tricky but it takes just a little time and patience.

Mix together the butter, parsley, tarragon, garlic, lemon and seasoning. Divide this among the four cavities and wrap each leg with 5 slices of bacon. Make sure that each end of bacon is on the underside of the leg.

Place the legs in a baking tray and roast in the oven for about 10 minutes – halfway through cooking, season the racks of rabbit, place them in the baking tray and cook alongside the legs. When the legs are crisp and golden brown, remove them from the the oven and rest for 5 minutes. This will give you enough time to cook your ravioli.

### TO FINISH

Cook the ravioli in boiling water for 3 minutes. Remove and place on kitchen towel. Heat 2 tablespoons of olive oil in a frying pan and fry the larger side of each ravioli until crispy.

As an optional garnish, put 1 tablespoon of butter in a heavy-based pan and fry the girolle mushrooms. When soft, add the baby leeks and asparagus and sauté for 1–2 minutes. Add the cherry tomatoes. Place the rabbit and ravioli on plates, scatter over the leek and asparagus mixture and garnish with a few fresh figs and sprigs of chervil. Serve immediately.

# RABBIT WITH SNAILS AND CHOCOLATE

**DAVID CUSPINERA, EDUARD PRADES AND JOAN RAMON GALINDO**

## SERVES 8

1.5kg edible live snails
(available from specialist
suppliers, such as www.
snailfarm.org.uk)
100ml olive oil
2 whole rabbits, jointed into
equal-sized portions (ask your
butcher to do this for you)
2 onions, peeled and diced
6 ripe tomatoes, finely chopped
1 dried chilli
100g spicy chorizo
50ml Cognac
2 garlic cloves
2 bay leaves
A few sprigs of thyme
2 litres beef stock
75g dark chocolate, grated
Salt and pepper

## FOR THE SNAILS

Wash the snails with water and discard any that are dead or don't look fresh. Put them in a pan of salted water and heat. Before the water begins to boil, drain off the hot water and refill the pan with fresh, cold water. Repeat this process three times. On the third change of water allow it to boil for 25 minutes. Drain the snails and reserve. (By changing the water, the snails are properly cleaned. It is important that the water doesn't boil during the first two stages as the snails will cook, retract into the shells and be hard to remove when eating.)

## FOR THE BRAISED RABBIT

In a heavy-based pan, heat a little of the oil and sear the rabbit pieces until browned. Remove from the pan and reserve. Add the remaining olive oil to the same pan and cook the onions over a low heat until they are soft and translucent. Add the tomatoes and dried chilli and cook for a further 5 minutes.

Add the rabbit, chorizo, Cognac, garlic, bay leaves and thyme and cook over a medium heat for 5–10 minutes. Add the snails and cook for a further 10 minutes, stirring occasionally. Add the beef stock, cover and cook over a low heat for about an hour. Sprinkle in the chocolate, stir thoroughly and cook for 10 minutes. Season to taste.

## TO SERVE

Serve in the pan on the table with some classic Spanish delicacies such as jamón, olives and fresh crusty bread.

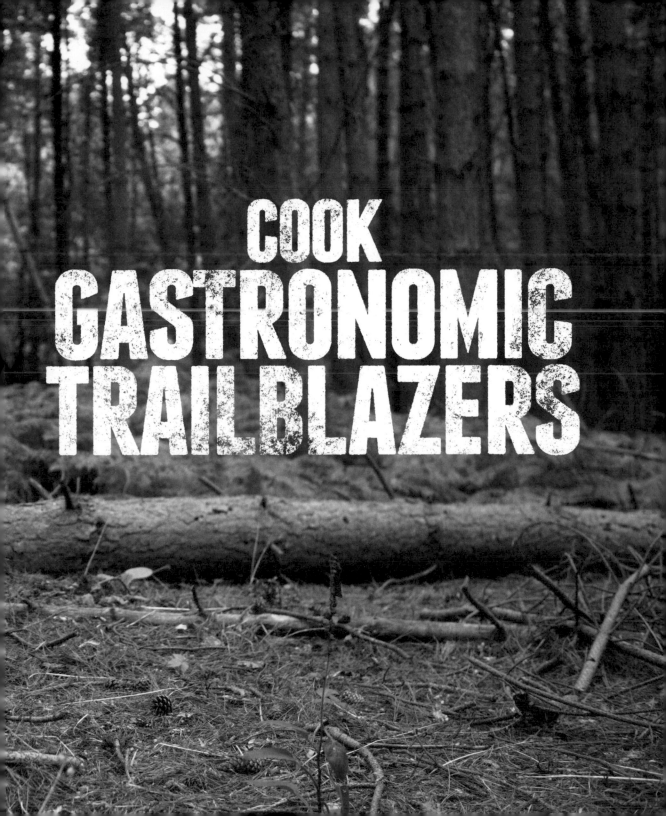

# COOK
# GASTRONOMIC
# TRAILBLAZERS

# BURYING THE LAMB

Roast lamb on a Sunday afternoon. Been there, done that. When a Mo Bro throws a Sunday lunch you can be sure he'll do it with style. Send the messenger pigeons far and wide, making sure to invite all your friends and family. Inviting everyone that you know means feeding everyone you know, and in some countries, running out of meat at a barbecue is tantamount to sacrilege and brings shame and dishonour to one's family. So how do you cook for 60–70 people and still have time to man the bar, whipping out your signature cocktail 'The Gentleman' for thirsty guests? Simple. Throw a whole lamb into a fire pit.

Dig a rather large hole in your backyard and light a mighty fire in the pit. Light another fire outside the pit as you will need this to put on top of the lamb so that hot coals are surrounding the carcass once you bury it. While the fire is burning, prepare the beast for the burial. Season your lamb generously and wrap it in a wet sheet – best check with your partner before sacrificing your bed linen. When the coals are hot, simply place the carcass on top, cover with more coals from your other fire and replace the earth, being sure to bury the lamb completely. The lamb will take about 8–9 hours to cook, during which time you can return to the decks, throw the DJ off and start mixing some fat beats.

# ROAST LOIN OF LAMB IN BREAD

## EVAN DOYLE

### SERVES 8

1.5kg organic plain flour
A good pinch of organic sea salt
2 x 400g portions of organic loin of lamb, with the belly still on (ask your butcher for these)
1 tablespoon organic wholegrain mustard
100g fresh pesto
2 sprigs of thyme, finely chopped
Organic sea salt and organic black pepper
100ml organic rapeseed oil

Preheat the oven to 220°C/gas mark 7. Place the flour and salt in a large bowl, making a depression in the centre, and slowly add 750ml cold water. Thoroughly mix the flour with the liquid, making sure all batter on the sides of the bowl is worked into the dough. Knead until you have a smooth dough and the sides of the bowl are clean. Cut it in half and set aside.

Place the lamb, skin-side down, and rub the mustard and half the pesto on the inside. Sprinkle over the chopped thyme and season with the salt and pepper. Wrap the belly around the lamb so the loin is completely covered. Roll and tie up with kitchen string. Heat a frying pan with the rapeseed oil. Seal the lamb on all sides, then put aside and cool for 5 minutes.

Roll out the two pieces of bread dough. Flour a medium-sized baking tray. Lay one half of the dough on the baking tray and place the two loins separately on top. Drizzle the remainder of the pesto over the lamb. Place the other half of dough over the lamb and, following the contours of the meat, press around the sides of the tray, making sure the lamb is fully sealed in. Put in the preheated oven and bake for 50 minutes.

### TO SERVE

When cooked, remove from the oven, set aside and let cool for 5 minutes. Cut around the lamb to carefully remove a bread lid. Take out the lamb, leaving the juices, and remove the kitchen string. Place the lamb back in the tray, replace the lid, and serve.

## SERVES 6

### SUCKLING PIG

2 large onions, peeled and chopped
2 carrots, peeled and chopped
3 celery sticks, chopped
2 garlic bulbs, halved
3 large sprigs of rosemary
1 shoulder of 16kg Tamworth (or similar) suckling pig, skin removed (ask your butcher to do this)
250ml mead honey wine (available from good spirit dealers)
1 tablespoon honey
½ cinnamon stick
1 clove
½ star anise
250ml chicken stock
Salt and pepper

### BOULANGERE POTATOES

2 onions, peeled and sliced
A sprig of rosemary
1.5kg King Edward potatoes, peeled and thinly sliced on a mandolin or with a sharp knife
3 garlic cloves, peeled and finely chopped
1 litre chicken stock
Olive oil for frying
Salt and pepper

### BABY VEGETABLES

8 young carrots
8 baby beetroot
8 Grelot onions
4 baby violet artichokes
Olive oil for roasting

### LEEK AND CEP GRATIN

125g butter
4 large leeks (white part only), washed and sliced thinly
300g cep mushrooms, sliced 1cm thick
30g flour
600ml milk
2 garlic cloves
50g Berkswell cheese, grated

# SLOW-ROAST TAMWORTH SUCKLING PIG SHOULDER, ROAST BABY VEGETABLES, LEEK AND CEP MUSHROOM GRATIN, BOULANGÈRE POTATOES

**JOHN TREMAYNE**

### FOR THE SUCKLING PIG

Preheat the oven to its highest setting. Put the chopped onions, carrots, celery, garlic and rosemary in a large roasting tray. Season the pork shoulder, lay it on the vegetables and roast in the hot oven for 15–20 minutes until golden brown. Reduce the temperature of the oven to 130°C/gas mark ½, cover the roasting tray with foil, making sure it is well sealed, and roast for 4 hours

Remove the foil and add to the roasting tray the mead honey wine, honey, cinnamon stick, clove, star anise and chicken stock. Roast uncovered for a further hour until the meat is falling off the bone. Once cooked, remove the tray from the oven and increase the oven temperature to 180°C/gas mark 4. Take the pork out of the tray and keep it warm. Pass the juice from the tray into a clean saucepan, place on the hob and reduce rapidly, skimming any scum and fat from the surface as it reduces. Put to one side.

### FOR THE BOULANGÈRE POTATOES

Place the sliced onions and rosemary in a pan and slowly cook in olive oil until soft and caramelised. Line an ovenproof pan with greaseproof paper, then layer in the thinly sliced potato with the caramelised onions and garlic. Pour over the chicken stock and season. Bake in the preheated oven for 50–60 minutes until the potatoes are cooked and nicely golden brown.

### FOR THE BABY VEGETABLES

Peel and trim the vegetables and place in a roasting tray with olive oil. Put in the oven with the Boulangère potatoes and cook for about 30 minutes until tender.

### FOR THE LEEK AND CEP GRATIN

Melt 50g butter in a saucepan, add the leeks and gently cook for 10 minutes until the leeks are soft but not coloured. Remove from the pan with a slotted spoon, place in a shallow ovenproof dish and set aside. In the same pan, add another 25g butter and melt. Sauté the ceps for 2–3 minutes until golden brown. Remove with a slotted spoon and add to the leeks. Then melt the remaining butter in the same pan, stir in the flour and cook on a low heat for 3 minutes to make a roux. Remove from the heat.

In a separate saucepan, heat the milk and garlic until just before boiling. Gradually stir into the roux, then return to the heat and bring to the boil, stirring until thickened. Pour over the leeks and ceps, sprinkle with cheese and cook in the oven, with the Boulangère potatoes, for 20–30 minutes or until golden.

### TO SERVE

Serve as a family feast in the middle of the table.

# PEAT-ROASTED ORGANIC BEEF FILLET

## EVAN DOYLE

Cooking with peat gives a wonderful earthy and slightly smoky taste that really suits beef. You also get pink, juicy roasted meat that allows you to brag about bringing true terroir to the kitchen. If you're lucky enough to live in Wales, Scotland or Ireland you should be able to readily find peat. For the adventurous Mo Bro who resides in cities, head to a garden centre where you can buy bags of peat – just make sure it is 'pure' peat that is 100% organic and free from additives, growth enhancers and chemicals ... just like your Mo.

### SERVES 8

1kg organic beef fillet
80g BrookLodge organic steak rub (or make you own with lots of pepper, salt and dried herbs such as thyme, rosemary and oregano)
50ml organic rapeseed oil
2kg 100% organic peat

Preheat the oven to 220°C/gas mark 7. Cut the beef fillet in half, rub in the BrookLodge steak rub and put to one side. Heat a large frying pan with the rapeseed oil and seal the beef on all sides to a nice brown colour.

In a large roasting tray, place enough of the peat to line the bottom of the dish (about a 2cm layer). On top, place both pieces of beef lengthways and cover with the rest of the peat, patting and pressing to form the shape of the meat. Put in the oven and roast for 20–25 minutes.

### TO SERVE

When cooked, remove from the oven, take the beef out of the peat and rub with some paper towel to take off most of the excess peat. Carve and serve.

'GIVE ME THE BEST THING YOU GOT AND STUFF IT WITH THE SECOND BEST THING YOU GOT'

MOE FROM *THE SIMPSONS* (ON A DATE AT SPRINGFIELD'S SNOOTIEST FRENCH RESTAURANT)

# CHANTERELLE-FILLED REINDEER FILLET WITH CRANBERRY SAUCE

## RISTO MIKKOLA

### SERVES 8

1.2kg reindeer fillet (or you could use venison fillet as an alternative), cut into 8 x 150g portions
4 yellow carrots, peeled and diced
4 purple carrots, peeled and diced
200g green beans, cut into batons
200g yellow beans, cut into batons
25ml olive oil, plus a little more for cooking
8 parsley stalks, chopped
Salt and pepper

### MUSHROOMS

320g Chanterelle mushrooms, finely chopped
80g onions, peeled and chopped
100g grated Swiss cheese
100g fresh white bread, cut into small pieces
4 sprigs of thyme
Oil for frying
Salt and pepper

### CRANBERRY SAUCE

50g onion, peeled and chopped
A sprig of thyme
130g butter
50g sugar
200g cranberries
Salt and pepper

### FOR THE MUSHROOMS

In a hot frying pan, sauté the mushrooms and onions in a little oil until soft and cooked through. Add the remaining ingredients and season with salt and pepper. Remove from the heat.

### FOR THE CRANBERRY SAUCE

In a frying pan, sauté the onion and thyme in 30g of the butter until soft and translucent. Add the sugar and allow to dissolve before adding the cranberries and 500ml water. Simmer for 10 minutes, remove from the heat and strain through a fine sieve. Return the sauce to the pan and gradually add the remaining butter a little at a time until incorporated. Season to taste with salt and pepper. Set aside in a warm place until serving.

### FOR THE REINDEER

Preheat the oven to 130°C/gas mark ½. Pierce the reindeer fillets lengthways with a sharp knife. Add a little olive oil to a hot frying pan and then sear the fillets for 1–2 minutes in batches until browned all over. Remove from the heat and set aside.

Fill each of the fillet cavities with the mushroom mix (use either a piping bag or spoon, or push it in with your fingers) and tightly wrap each fillet in a 30cm square of tin foil. Place in the oven and roast for 10 minutes. Remove from the oven and rest the meat for a further 5 minutes.

Bring a saucepan of lightly salted water to the boil and blanch the carrots and beans for 3 minutes. Transfer to a bowl and lightly toss with the oil and parsley. Remove the foil from the reindeer and cut into 1cm slices.

### TO SERVE

On a large platter, arrange the vegetables and slices of meat and get stylish with the cranberry sauce. Serve immediately.

# CRAYFISH

## RISTO MIKKOLA

### SERVES 8

1 bunch of dill
50g sea salt
200g sugar
8 crayfish

In your backyard sauna, put 5 litres of water in a very large cooking pot, add the dill, salt and sugar, and bring to a boil. Add the crayfish and cook for 6–8 minutes, until the shells turn red. Then remove from the heat and leave to cool in the broth until they are cool enough to handle.

### TO SERVE

Eat immediately whilst sweating profusely.

# COOK POULTRY AND GAME

# CHERMOULA SPRING CHICKEN, GRILLED ROMERO PEPPERS, ALMOND COUSCOUS, CORIANDER GREEK YOGURT

DEON JANSEN

### SERVES 6

6 Romero peppers
6 spatchcock spring chickens (ask your butcher to prepare the birds this way)

### CORIANDER GREEK YOGURT

A small bunch of coriander, chopped
200g Greek yogurt
Juice of ½ lemon
Salt and cracked black pepper

### COUSCOUS

100g flaked almonds
600g couscous
50ml olive oil
Juice of 1 lemon
Salt and pepper

### CHERMOULA SPICE

Juice of 1 lemon
1 teaspoon whole cumin
1 teaspoon smoked paprika
1 red chilli, deseeded and chopped
A small bunch of coriander, chopped
2 garlic cloves, peeled
Olive oil

### FOR THE PEPPERS

Place the peppers on top of the gas burners until they turn black (if you don't have gas burners, a barbecue will do just as well). Remove from the flames and place the cooked peppers in a bowl, cover with cling film and steam for 10 minutes (this will allow the skin to peel away from the flesh). Under running water, peel off the blackened, blistered skin – don't be too fussy as the burnt bits will have a rich, smoky flavour. Set aside until serving.

### FOR THE YOGURT

Mix all the ingredients together in a bowl. This can be done a few hours before serving and kept in the fridge.

### FOR THE COUSCOUS

Toast the almonds under the grill until they turn golden brown. Place the couscous in a bowl and add the olive oil, lemon juice and seasoning. Mix together, then add enough boiling water to cover the couscous. Cover with cling film and steam for 20 minutes. Remove the cling film, fluff with a fork and add the toasted almonds.

### FOR THE CHERMOULA SPICE

Place all the ingredients in a food processor and blitz, adding enough olive oil to make a wet marinade.

### FOR THE SPRING CHICKEN

Preheat the oven to 200°C/gas mark 6. Liberally cover the birds with the chermoula spice (you can do this the day before) and roast in an ovenproof dish for 15 minutes, or until cooked. The leg bone should be easy to remove once cooked.

### TO SERVE

Spoon the couscous onto the plates. Divide the peppers between the plates and place a chicken in the middle. Finish with a dollop of coriander yogurt.

# CHICKEN WITH MOREL MUSHROOMS

**DUNCAN MAGUIRE**

## SERVES 6

40g dried morels
6 chicken breasts, skin on,
preferably a grain-fed and
free-range bird
Sea salt and freshly ground
black pepper
25g unsalted butter
1 tablespoon olive oil
200ml dry white wine
2 tablespoons crème fraîche
1 tablespoon redcurrant jelly
A few sprigs of fresh
redcurrants to garnish

Soak the morels for 15 minutes in just enough boiling water to cover them. Remove the morels from the liquid and drain the liquid through a fine sieve to remove any grit. Reserve both morels and liquid.

Preheat the oven to 150°C/gas mark 2. Season the chicken breasts well. In a heavy frying pan large enough for all the chicken, heat the butter and oil over a medium heat. Add the chicken breasts and fry for 5 minutes on each side until nicely browned. Then drain off any fat, and add the morel soaking liquid, the morels and the white wine. Simmer uncovered for 10 minutes until the chicken is cooked through.

Transfer the chicken to serving plates. In the frying pan, stir in the crème fraîche and the redcurrant jelly, bring to the boil and cook for 2 minutes. Pour the sauce over the chicken breasts and serve topped with the redcurrants.

'I COOK WITH WINE.
SOMETIMES I EVEN ADD
IT TO THE FOOD'

W. C. FIELDS

# CHICKEN PIE, MASH AND GREEN BEANS

## WOLFE CONYNGHAM

### SERVES 6

½ cooked chicken
1 onion, peeled and chopped
100g smoked streaky bacon,
cut into little pieces
25g mushrooms, sliced
70g butter
30g plain flour
200ml chicken stock
225ml milk
2 tablespoons cream cheese
1 packet of ready-rolled puff
pastry
1 egg, beaten
1kg potatoes, peeled
1kg green beans, ends trimmed
Extra-virgin olive oil
Salt and pepper

Preheat the oven to 200°C/gas mark 6. Strip the carcass of chicken, cutting the meat into large pieces. (If you prefer, you can buy uncooked chicken but you would need to precook it at this stage.)

In a pan, sauté the onion, bacon and mushrooms in 20g butter and 1 tablespoon olive oil. When softened, add the flour and stir. Add the chicken stock, stirring continuously. Then add 125ml of the milk and the cream cheese to make the sauce rich and creamy. If the sauce is a bit too thick, add a little water. Add the precooked chicken and stir carefully until the meat is completely coated.

Transfer the contents of the pan to a large pie dish. Cover with the pastry, making a vent in the pie top. Use your Movember cookie cutter to add some Mo styling to the pie (see image below) and brush the pie crust with the beaten egg. Put the pie in the oven and bake for around 25 minutes or until golden.

For the mash, boil the potatoes in salted water until cooked. Drain, allow to steam for 5 minutes, then mash thoroughly. Heat the remaining milk and butter in a saucepan and stir through the mashed potatoes. Season to taste.

Blanch the green beans in salted boiling water until cooked. Drain and toss with a little extra-virgin olive oil. Season to taste.

# ROAST PHEASANT WITH SAVOY CABBAGE, CHICORY AND CRISPY PANCETTA

DAVE BONE

## SERVES 4

250ml red wine
50ml port
500ml veal stock
1 pheasant (ask your butcher to remove the legs and wings but keep the breasts on the frame)
100ml olive oil
6 sprigs of thyme
4 garlic cloves
2 heads of chicory (endive), sliced lengthways
6 shallots, peeled
4 slices pancetta
½ head Savoy cabbage, cut into 2.5cm slices
Salt and pepper

Preheat the oven to 180°C/gas mark 4.

### FOR THE SAUCE

In a heavy-based saucepan, reduce the wine and port over a low heat until you are left with about 100ml of liquid. Add 450ml of the veal stock and gently reduce until you have a rich sauce. Set aside until serving.

### FOR THE PHEASANT

Season the pheasant with salt and pepper. In a hot frying pan, heat 2–3 tablespoons olive oil and fry the pheasant legs and breasts for about 5 minutes until golden all over. Transfer to a baking tray, add the thyme and 3 garlic cloves, and bake for 25 minutes. Remove from the oven but keep the oven on.

### FOR THE CHICORY AND PANCETTA

In a hot ovenproof frying pan, heat 1 tablespoon olive oil, place the chicory face down and gently fry for 3 minutes. Add the remaining garlic clove and all the shallots. Sauté for a further 2 minutes before adding the remaining veal stock and transferring to the oven for 15 minutes. Remove (but keep the oven on) and set aside until serving.

Line an oven tray with greaseproof paper and place the pancetta slices on top. Bake in the oven for 25 minutes or until crisp. Remove and turn the oven off.

### FOR THE CABBAGE

Bring a large saucepan of water to the boil. Blanch the cabbage for 2 minutes and drain. In a separate pan, gently heat about 2 tablespoons olive oil and toss the cabbage through with a little salt and pepper.

### TO SERVE

Place the cabbage on a wooden chopping board and add the pheasant, chicory, shallots and pancetta. Pour the sauce into a small jug or saucepan and serve.

'ANY MAN WITH A MOUSTACHE AND SHOTGUN SHOULD BE REFERRED TO AS "SIR"'

# PAN-FRIED QUAIL WITH ROASTED PUMPKIN AND HAZELNUTS

## DAVID JOHNSON

### SERVES 6

¼ pumpkin, peeled, deseeded and chopped into 1cm squares
1 banana shallot, peeled and sliced into thin rings
70ml white wine vinegar
70ml extra-virgin rapeseed oil
70ml hazelnut oil
100g hazelnuts, toasted and roughly chopped
6 whole quails, jointed (ask your butcher to do this for you)
Salt and cracked black pepper
2 bunches of watercress, picked and washed
A handful of chervil, picked
Olive oil for frying

Heat a little olive oil in a heavy-based frying pan. Add the diced pumpkin and sauté over a medium heat until just cooked. In a small bowl, marinate the shallot rings in 20ml of the vinegar and 10ml of the rapeseed oil. Set aside until serving. In another bowl, whisk the remainder of the vinegar and rapeseed oil and all of the hazelnut oil. Mix in 30g of the chopped hazelnuts and set aside.

Heat a heavy-based frying pan with a little oil until very hot. Season the quail pieces with salt and pepper and pan-fry until golden and the skin is crispy.

### TO SERVE

Coat the watercress leaves with the oil and vinegar dressing and scatter over the plates. Add the warm pumpkin pieces and marinated shallot rings. Place the roasted quail pieces on top of the salad, drizzle with some more of the dressing, and sprinkle over the remainder of the chopped hazelnuts and the chervil.

# COOK
# FISH

# SUSTAINABLE WHITE FISH CEVICHE WITH EDAMAME BEANS

SIMON FERNANDEZ

Ceviche is a seafood dish with roots in Peruvian cuisine. It is a great way to eat fresh fish and its flavours lend themselves really well to sustainable fish stocks. This dish also draws from Asian cookery.

## SERVES 6–8

350g sustainable white fish, such as coley or pollack, diced into 1cm pieces
15g chives, finely chopped
15g coriander leaves, torn
100ml coconut cream
20g ginger, peeled and finely grated
Juice and zest of 1 lemon
Juice of 2 limes
500g edamame beans
Sea salt flakes
1 avocado, peeled and finely diced (add a squeeze of lemon juice to stop oxidation)
1 tablespoon fish sauce

## TO GARNISH

5g chopped chives
Tips and fronds of 1 fennel bulb

Mix the diced fish with the chives and coriander, and store in a sealed container in the fridge for at least 2 hours. In a saucepan, bring the coconut cream and ginger to the boil, then simmer for a few minutes until reduced by half. Remove from the heat and set aside to cool.

Marinate the fish with the citrus juice and zest for 20 minutes (although anything between 15–45 minutes is fine). Drop the edamame (shells on) into a pan of salted boiling water for 4 minutes. Drain in a colander and transfer to a bowl of cold water (so they retain their colour). Set aside.

## TO SERVE

Add the edamame to boiling water for 1 minute, then drain through a colander, place in a large bowl and sprinkle with sea salt flakes. Drain the juice from the fish by squeezing through a fine sieve. Transfer the fish to a separate bowl, combine with the coconut sauce and avocado, and season with fish sauce to taste. Put the ceviche in serving bowls, garnish with chives and fennel fronds, and serve with chopsticks.

# GRILLED SARDINE FILLETS PROVENÇAL

RICHARD ROBINSON

## SERVES 4

400g courgettes, cut at an angle
into 1cm slices
Sea salt
6 sardines, filleted
Olive oil
Black pepper
Balsamic vinegar

## SHELLFISH VINAIGRETTE

12 fresh cockles, cleaned
12 fresh mussels, cleaned
A pinch of saffron threads
½ garlic clove, peeled
1 tablespoon red wine vinegar
4 tablespoons olive oil
15g fresh tarragon, chopped
Salt and pepper

## TO SERVE

120g sauce vierge (see page 182)

Sprinkle the courgette slices with sea salt and leave for 1 hour over a wire rack or sieve (this will bring the excess moisture out). Dry thoroughly with a cloth but do not wash.

For the shellfish vinaigrette, put 50ml water in a saucepan and bring to the boil. Add the cleaned cockles and mussels, cover and steam until the shells open. Remove the shellfish and reserve the cooking liquor. Remove the shellfish from the shells, put in a bowl and set aside.

In a small pan, add the saffron and the reserved shellfish cooking liquor. Bring to the boil and bubble to reduce by half. Stir in the garlic, red wine vinegar and olive oil. Then cool.

Add the tarragon to the shellfish and mix with the cooled vinaigrette. Season to taste and set aside.

Place the courgette slices in a very hot, dry pan. Sear until nicely golden on both sides. Remove from the heat and toss with olive oil and black pepper.

Preheat the grill to hot. Brush both sides of the sardine fillets generously with olive oil and season well. Put on a grill tray and cook under the grill, skin-side up for 3–4 minutes until crisp, golden and the fillets are cooked.

### TO SERVE

Put 3 sardine fillets on each plate, spoon over the sauce vierge and drizzle with a little shellfish vinaigrette.

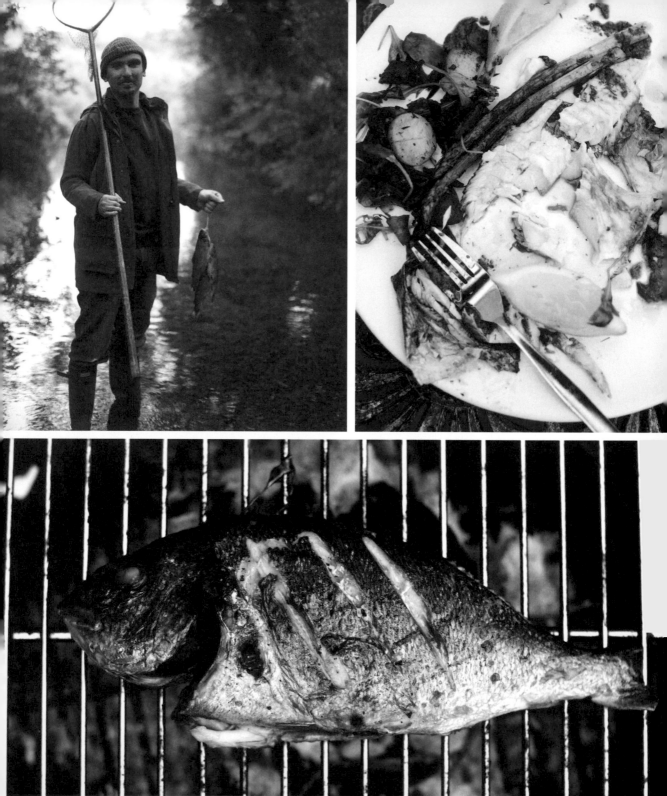

# GRILLED WHOLE BLACK BREAM, TUSCAN POTATOES, ASPARAGUS AND SALSA VERDE

SAM WILSON

## SERVES 8

8 small black bream, scaled and cleaned
2 bunches of asparagus, ends trimmed and peeled
Salt and pepper

## TUSCAN POTATOES

1kg new potatoes
30g butter
60ml olive oil
2 red onions, peeled and cut into wedges
50g fresh rosemary, picked and chopped
50g fresh oregano, picked and chopped
4 garlic cloves, peeled and sliced
200g rocket, picked and washed
100g semi-sundried tomatoes

## SALSA VERDE

A small bunch of chives, picked and washed
A small bunch of tarragon, picked and washed
A small bunch of dill, picked and washed
A small bunch of parsley, picked and washed
2 small bunches of basil, picked and washed
50g capers
50g cornichons
5 garlic cloves
30g Dijon mustard
300ml olive oil

### FOR THE TUSCAN POTATOES

In a pan of salted water, bring the potatoes to the boil. Reduce the heat and simmer until half-cooked. Strain, set aside and allow to cool.

In a large frying pan, melt the butter with the oil, then add the potatoes and onions and cook until golden brown. Add the rosemary, oregano and garlic and cook for 5 minutes on a medium heat. Remove and toss through the rocket and sundried tomatoes. Set aside.

### FOR THE SALSA VERDE

Make sure the herbs are dry and place all the salsa verde ingredients, except the olive oil, in a blender and blitz, pouring in the oil slowly until you have a bright green, wet sauce. Season to taste with salt and pepper.

### FOR THE BREAM AND ASPARAGUS

Heat the barbecue or griddle. Score the bream with a sharp knife across the flesh 3 times on each side and season with salt and pepper. Cook on the barbecue or griddle for 5 minutes on each side. When the fish is nearly cooked, lightly oil and season the asparagus and chargrill on the barbecue or griddle for a few minutes.

### TO SERVE

On each plate, add the Tuscan potatoes, fish and asparagus, drizzle with salsa verde and serve immediately.

'FISH, TO TASTE RIGHT, MUST
SWIM THREE TIMES – IN WATER,
IN BUTTER AND IN WINE'

POLISH PROVERB

# SALT CRUST BAKED WILD SEA BREAM

EVAN DOYLE

## SERVES 8

4 whole, wild, line-caught sea
bream, about 400-500g each
4kg organic sea salt
8 egg whites
4 lemons, thinly sliced
2 fennel bulbs, thinly sliced
200ml Irish organic
rapeseed oil

Remove the scales, gut and clean the sea bream
(or get your fishmonger to do this for you).

Preheat the oven to 220°C/gas mark 7. In a large
bowl, mix together the sea salt and egg whites
and put to one side. Stuff some of the sliced
lemon and fennel inside the cavities of the fish.

Using 2 roasting trays, line the bottoms with half
of the sea salt mixture. Add the rest of the fennel
and lemon on top, then place 2 sea bream in
each tray. Drizzle with the organic rapeseed oil
and cover with the rest of the sea salt mixture
and pack down. Put in the oven and roast for
30 minutes.

## TO SERVE

When cooked, set aside for 10 minutes. Then,
using a rolling pin, hit the salt crust to crack it,
then lift off the salt crust. Carefully lift out the
sea bream, remove the flesh from the bones
and serve.

'DRESSING IMPECCABLY WITH BRACES AND A HUGE MOUSTACHE IS SAID TO BRING ANGLERS LUCK'

# ROASTED SALMON, SAMPHIRE, ASPARAGUS AND CHERRY TOMATOES WITH LEMON DILL DRESSING

**DEON JANSEN**

## SERVES 6

6 x 160g salmon fillets, skin removed
400g asparagus spears, trimmed, sliced lengthways
300g samphire (available from good fishmongers or your local beach)
200g vine-ripened cherry tomatoes, halved
Olive oil for frying
Salt and pepper

## DRESSING

2 garlic cloves, peeled and finely chopped
Juice of 1 lemon
150ml extra-virgin olive oil
¼ bunch dill, chopped
1 red chilli, deseeded and finely diced

To make the dressing, combine all the ingredients in a mixing bowl and allow the flavours to infuse. This can be made a few hours in advance.

Heat a frying pan until hot. At the same time, bring a saucepan of salted water to the boil. Add the cooking oil to the frying pan and season the salmon fillets with salt and pepper. Fry the salmon fillets until just cooked, you want them to be slightly undercooked in the middle. Remove from the pan and set aside.

Place the asparagus in the pan of boiling water for 20 seconds. Add the samphire to the pan and cook for a further 10 seconds.

## TO SERVE

Drain the vegetables well and divide between 6 serving plates. Add the halved tomatoes and gently place a salmon fillet on each plate. Drizzle over the dressing and enjoy.

'A WELL-GROOMED MOUSTACHE IS THE KEY TO MANY GREAT OUTFITS AND AN ESSENTIAL INGREDIENT AT A MOVEMBER DINNER PARTY. NO MO – NO GO'

# HERB-CRUSTED JOHN DORY WITH A CURRIED MUSSEL BROTH

**IVAN VARIAN**

## SERVES 6

150g white bread
A handful of basil
A handful of parsley
Zest of 1 lemon
500g mussels
2 shallots, peeled and sliced
A sprig of thyme
A bay leaf
2 glasses dry white wine
1 medium onion, peeled and finely diced
1 celery stick, finely diced
1 carrot, peeled and finely diced
1 tablespoon curry powder
A pinch of saffron
450ml Noilly Prat vermouth
450ml fish stock
200ml double cream
Olive oil
6 John Dory fillets
Salt and pepper

Break up the bread and place it in a blender with the basil, parsley, lemon zest, some salt and pepper and a glug of olive oil. Blitz for a few minutes until it becomes fine crumbs. Put to one side.

Scrub the mussels with a wire brush to get the gunk off. Use the back of a knife to remove any barnacles and remove the hairy, wispy bit that's technically known as the 'beard', but for this recipe we shall call it the 'Mo'. Discard any mussels that don't close when tapped or else they may be the last shellfish you and your guests are brave enough to eat.

Place a large, heavy-based pan on a high heat and pour in a bit of olive oil, the sliced shallots, the sprig of thyme and the bay leaf. Fry until the shallots are softened. Turn up the heat to its highest setting and add the mussels along with a glass of white wine – and have a glass yourself. Put the lid on and give the pan a shake. Cook for 3–4 minutes or until the mussels have opened. Remove from the heat and take the mussel meat from the shells. Discard the shells and any mussels that haven't opened, while keeping both the mussel meat and the cooking liquor that remains in the pan.

On a medium heat, pour some olive oil in a pan and add the diced onion, celery and carrot. Season with salt and pepper and cook until nicely softened. Add the curry powder and saffron and stir. Pour in the Noilly Prat, turn up the heat and boil until the liquid has reduced by half. Then add the fish stock and the cooking juices from the mussels. Reduce the liquid again by half and then stir in the cream and add the mussel meat. Cook for 1 minute, remove from the heat and set aside.

Heat a large frying pan and get it smoking hot. Add a touch of olive oil and then add your John Dory fillets, skin-side down. Season with salt and pepper. Press down on the fillets to stop them curling up and cook for 2–3 minutes. Flip them over and cook for a minute on the flesh side. Place them on a grill tray, skin-side down. Pat your breadcrumb mix on the flesh side of the fish – if it's too crumbly, add more olive oil. Place under a medium grill for a few minutes until the crust goes nicely golden, but watch it like a hawk or else it'll burn.

## TO SERVE

Pour the mussel broth into shallow bowls and place the fish on top. Serve to your guests with a swagger and a twirl of your Mo.

# FISH STEW WITH SNAPPER, MONKFISH, BRAISED FENNEL AND SAFFRON AIOLI

## TROY MAGUIRE

This recipe has quite a few elements to it but the results are worth it! Serve this at your dinner party and humbly accept praise and applause like this is just one of your specialities in an arsenal of killer dishes.

## SERVES 8

4 large onions, peeled and chopped
1 leek, white part only, chopped
1 celery heart, chopped
2 garlic cloves, chopped
1 red chilli
2 bay leaves
4 star anise
3kg monkfish bones (ask your fishmonger for these)
½ bottle of white wine
2 shots of Pernod
2 x 400g cans good-quality tomatoes
3 fennel bulbs, quartered
Fish or chicken stock
A few knobs of butter
1kg mussels
1kg monkfish fillets, cut into small chunks
3 langoustines
1kg red snapper, filleted and cut into large pieces
Olive oil

## AIOLI

A pinch of saffron strands
Juice of 1 lemon
¼ teaspoon smoked paprika
3 egg yolks
1 teaspoon Dijon mustard
½ teaspoon chopped garlic
300ml olive oil
Salt and pepper

## FOR THE SOUP BASE

Sweat the chopped onions, leek, celery and garlic in olive oil until translucent. Add the chilli, bay leaves and 2 star anise, and sweat for a further 20 minutes. Add the fish bones, white wine and Pernod. Then add the tomatoes, cover with a little water if necessary, and cook for 2 hours on a low heat. Discard the bones, blitz with a soup blender, sieve and set aside.

## FOR THE BRAISED FENNEL

Heat the butter in a deep frying pan and cook the fennel for a few minutes until light golden. Add 250ml fish or chicken stock, a little extra butter and 2 star anise. Reduce the heat, cover and simmer for about 30 minutes until really tender.

## FOR THE AIOLI

Soak the saffron in the lemon juice for 5 minutes, then add the paprika, egg yolks, Dijon mustard and garlic. Whisk in the olive oil a little at a time until the mixture starts to thicken. Season and mix in a tablespoon of water.

## TO FINISH

Heat the fish soup base in a large saucepan until nearly boiling, then add the mussels, cover and cook for 3–4 minutes until the shells have opened. Discard any that don't open. Meanwhile, in a separate pan, fry the monkfish fillets, langoustines and snapper for about 3–4 minutes, turning over a medium heat until cooked and the flesh is just starting to flake. Place the fish on top of the fennel, pour over the fish soup and serve with aioli and toasted crusty bread slices.

# SMOKED HADDOCK RISOTTO, SOFT-BOILED QUAIL EGGS, PARSNIP CRISPS

NICK BUTLER

**SERVES 6**

**QUAIL EGGS**

12 quail eggs

**PARSNIP CRISPS**

1 large parsnip
Oil for deep-frying

**RISOTTO**

2 litres chicken stock
2 sprigs of thyme
20 black peppercorns
1 bay leaf
50ml olive oil
2 shallots, peeled and finely diced
600g Arborio rice
3 pinches of salt
500ml white wine
250g smoked haddock fillet, skinned and diced
500ml milk
100g frozen peas
50g butter
50g grated Parmesan
¼ bunch of parsley, finely chopped
Pea shoots to garnish (optional)

## FOR THE QUAIL EGGS

Prepare a container of iced water. Bring a pan of water to the boil and carefully put the eggs in the pan. Boil for 1 minute and 25 seconds exactly. Remove with a slotted spoon and transfer straight into the iced water. When cooled completely, gently peel the shells and set the eggs aside until serving. If you are having trouble peeling the eggs, place them in white wine vinegar for 1 hour; this will make them easier to peel as the vinegar will break down the shell.

## FOR THE PARSNIP CRISPS

Peel the outer skin of the parsnip and discard. Then draw a vegetable peeler down the length of the parsnip to make thin ribbons. Heat a pan of oil to 140°C or until a cube of bread goes golden in 1 minute 30 seconds; do not make it too hot or the crisps will burn. Place the strips of parsnip in the hot oil for around 45 seconds. Remove and drain on kitchen paper. The parsnips should be a light golden brown colour – any darker and they will taste bitter. These can be made the day before and stored in an airtight container.

## FOR THE RISOTTO

Put the chicken stock in a saucepan with the thyme, peppercorns and bay leaf and bring to the boil. Then remove from the heat and leave for 30 minutes. Remove the peppercorns, bay and thyme and return to the pan. Bring back to the boil and keep on a low heat.

Put the olive oil in a separate large saucepan, add the shallots and cook, without colouring, until translucent. Add the rice with the salt and cook for 1 minute. Pour in the wine and reduce until the rice has absorbed the wine and the mixture is almost dry. Add enough of the chicken stock to cover the rice and simmer for a few minutes, stirring continuously until the stock has been absorbed. Continue doing this, adding more stock until the rice is almost cooked, for about 20 minutes. Meanwhile, in a separate saucepan, lightly poach the diced smoked haddock in the milk for 3–4 minutes. This will soften the texture and give great flavour to the milk.

When the rice is cooked but still slightly firm to the tooth, add 100ml of the haddock milk and continue stirring for 2 minutes. Add the diced smoked haddock and the frozen peas. Continue stirring until the smoked haddock and peas are cooked. When both are cooked, add the butter and grated Parmesan and stir thoroughly. Add the parsley at the last minute – the risotto should be creamy and a little soup-like.

## TO SERVE

Spoon a portion of risotto into each bowl. Cut the quail eggs in half and place 4 halves around each plate. Garnish with the parsnip crisps, pea shoots and serve immediately.

# SEARED RIVER TROUT WITH APPLE PURÉE, HERBED FENNEL SALAD AND SALSA AGRESTO

**SAM WILSON**

Trout, recognised as the world's only freshwater game fish, is known as the 'gentleman of the river'. It goes well with salsa agresto, a traditional Italian sauce made from herbs, nuts, verjuice and oil. Here we use Chardonnay vinegar instead of the acidic verjuice as it is more readily available.

## SERVES 6

6 trout fillets (ask your
fishmonger to pin bone
and trim)
1-2 tablepoons oil for cooking

## APPLE PURÉE

6 Pink Lady apples, peeled and
diced
2 shallots, peeled and diced
2 tablespoons crème fraîche
Juice from ½ lemon
Salt and ground white pepper

## SALSA AGRESTO

125g toasted walnuts
125g toasted almonds
1 garlic clove, peeled and
chopped
½ bunch of parsley, chopped
¼ bunch of basil, chopped
300ml olive oil
Salt and pepper
Chardonnay vinegar

## HERBED FENNEL SALAD

1 fennel bulb, cut in half and
sliced as finely as you can with
a sharp knife
A bunch of dill, chopped
A bunch of chives, chopped
½ bunch of chervil, chopped
30ml olive oil
Juice from ½ lemon

## FOR THE APPLE PURÉE

Place the apples and shallots in a saucepan. Cover with water and cook until tender. Remove from the heat and allow to cool. Transfer to a food processor and blend into a purée, while slowly adding the crème fraîche. Transfer to a separate bowl, add the lemon juice and seasoning to taste. Set aside until serving.

## FOR THE SALSA AGRESTO

Place the toasted walnuts and almonds in a blender and lightly blitz. Empty into a mixing bowl, add the chopped garlic, parsley, basil and olive oil, and mix together. Season to taste with salt and pepper and a little Chardonnay vinegar.

## FOR THE FENNEL SALAD

In a mixing bowl, combine the finely sliced fennel and chopped herbs with the olive oil and lemon juice.

## TO SERVE

In a medium hot pan, add the oil, then fry the trout fillets in batches skin-side down until the skin is crispy. This should take 3–4 minutes. Remove from the heat and turn the fillets over to finish cooking for a further 2 minutes. Place on kitchen paper to remove excess oil.

On 6 plates, place a smear of the apple purée. Divide the salad evenly between the dishes and put a fillet of trout on each. Spoon on the salsa agresto and serve.

# SALMON SASHIMI AND SALMON SUSHI

**DUNCAN MAGUIRE**

When fishing for salmon, a strong masculine jib and gentlemanly air will have fish jumping into the net. Here raw salmon is prepared for the popular Japanese dishes of sashimi and sushi.

## SERVES 8

### RICE

1 tablespoon sugar
A pinch of salt
2 tablespoons rice wine
vinegar
400g short-grain rice,
rinsed in cold water
and drained well
Tezu seasoning

### SALMON SASHIMI

1.5kg side of fresh salmon,
pin boned and skinned
(ask your fishmonger to do
this)

### SUSHI

Remaining salmon fillet
Wasabi

### TO SERVE

100g pickled ginger root
(available from Asian
grocers)
1 small daikon root
(available from Asia
grocers), shredded
30g wasabi paste
100ml soy sauce

### FOR THE RICE

In a small bowl, dissolve the sugar and salt in the vinegar. Set aside.

Place the rice and 1 litre water in a heavy-bottomed saucepan with a lid, bring to the boil, reduce the heat to a simmer and cook for 10–15 minutes, or until all the water has been absorbed by the rice. Resist lifting the lid until the rice is cooked – to check if the water has been absorbed, gently tilt the saucepan on its side whilst carefully holding on the lid. If liquid tips out, return to the heat and cook for a few minutes longer. Alternatively, place the rice and water in a rice cooker and turn on. The cooker will turn off when it's cooked.

When the rice is cooked and still hot, transfer to a large bowl and mix in the Tezu seasoning. Use a cutting and folding action with a spatula and be careful not to break the grains of rice to avoid it becoming sludgy and pasty. You could make the rice ahead of time, and put it to one side, covered with a damp cloth to keep it moist.

### FOR THE SALMON SASHIMI

Trim the side of salmon into a long rectangle shape, cutting away any white fatty parts from the belly. The remaining fish should have the grain running diagonally across the fillet.

Cut the fillet in half across the middle. Reserve half for the sushi recipe. Slice at right angles across the fillet so you have equal bite-sized pieces about 1cm thick. Use a very sharp knife and slice cleanly through the fish in one action; never use a sawing motion as this will crush the cells of the flesh and affect the taste and texture. Set aside.

### FOR THE SUSHI

With slightly wet hands (to prevent the rice sticking), gently press a small amount of rice between your palm and the first 2 fingers of your other hand to form a small brick. Smear a little wasabi over the topside of the brick.

Cut thin slices from the salmon fillet, cutting across the grain. Drape one thin slice of the salmon over the topside of the rice.

### TO SERVE

On a plate, arrange the sashimi slices in a fan and place the sushi next to it in a way that would please Mr Miyagi. Place a small amount of the pickled ginger, shredded daikon and wasabi on the plate. In a side dish, pour a little of the soy sauce and serve. Itadakimasu.

# COOK
# DESSERTS

# BAKED APPLES WITH CRÈME FRAÎCHE

**DAVID JOHNSON**

## SERVES 6

75g ground almonds
15ml honey
15g demerara sugar
25ml apple brandy
85g sultanas
½ teaspoon ground cinnamon
60g softened butter
45g chopped apricots
6 apples
Crème fraîche to serve

Mix all the ingredients together, except the apples, and leave to soak at room temperature for 1 hour. Preheat the oven to 180°C/gas mark 4. Core the apples and put in an ovenproof dish. Fill the apple cavities with the sultana mixture, spooning a little extra on top and reserving the leftover mixture for the sauce. Bake in the oven for 20–25 minutes until the apples are soft but not collapsing. Pour the excess mixture into a small pan, bring it to the boil and stir until the mixture has thickened.

## TO SERVE

Place the apples on a large plate and pour over the extra sauce. Serve with crème fraîche.

'COOKING SHOULD BE AN ENJOYABLE EXPERIENCE – IT'S NOT ROCKET SCIENCE'

# RASPBERRY MERINGUES, ROASTED PEACHES AND VANILLA MASCARPONE

**DEON JANSEN**

## SERVES 6

400g mascarpone cheese
4 drops of vanilla extract (not essence) or the seeds of 1 vanilla pod
60g icing sugar
6 ripe peaches
6 meringues (bought from a good bakery)
180g raspberries

In a bowl, mix the mascarpone, vanilla and half the icing sugar. Set aside. Cut the peaches in half and remove the stones. Place on an oven tray and dust with some of the remaining icing sugar. Grill under a medium heat for about 10 minutes until soft and caramelised.

## TO SERVE

Place a meringue on each plate and spoon on the mascarpone. Arrange 2 peach halves per plate, drizzle on any roasting juices from the peaches, and garnish with the raspberries and a dusting of icing sugar.

# BLUEBERRY, APPLE AND VICTORIA PLUM CRUMBLE, MINT YOGURT

**JAMES LYON-SHAW**

## SERVES 6

350g Bramley apples, peeled, cored and sliced
Juice of 1 lemon
100g caster sugar
750g Victoria plums, cored, stones removed and halved
200g blueberries
100g self-raising flour
1 teaspoon cinnamon
1 teaspoon ground cardamom
50g butter, diced, plus a little extra for greasing
50g golden caster sugar
4 tablespoons milk
1 egg, beaten
50g pecans, crushed
500ml natural yogurt
6 mint leaves

Preheat the oven to 160°C/gas mark 3. Butter an ovenproof dish liberally. Place the sliced apples, lemon juice and caster sugar in a pan and bring to the boil. Cover and cook on a medium heat for 5 minutes, then add the halved plums and cook for a further 2 minutes. Pour the cooked fruit into the buttered dish, sprinkle over the blueberries, and stir in well.

In a mixing bowl, add the flour, cinnamon, cardamom and diced butter and rub together. Add the sugar, milk and egg and mix to a soft batter. Place in the fridge for 30 minutes to set. Then roll the dough into a 5cm cylinder, wrap in cling film and return to the fridge for 30 minutes to firm up.

When set, take out of the fridge and remove the cling film. Then slice it into discs and lay on top of the fruit in the baking dish, leaving a small gap between each one. Sprinkle over the crushed pecans. Cook for 25 minutes until the top is golden. Serve with the yogurt and ripped-up mint leaves.

'THERE IS A TERM "MISE EN PLACE" – IT'S PART OF EVERY CHEF'S VOCABULARY. IN FRENCH, IT LITERALLY MEANS EVERYTHING IN PLACE. GET READY; GET SET UP AND GET ON WITH IT'

# CRÊPES SUZETTE

## DUNCAN MAGUIRE

A blowtorch will come in handy for this classic pancakes recipe with
a boozy orange sauce.

### SERVES 6

### CRÊPES

125g plain flour
15g caster sugar
A pinch of salt
2 medium free-range eggs
300ml milk
25g butter, melted

### SAUCE

100g unsalted butter
100g caster sugar, plus extra for
sprinkling
Juice of 1 mandarin
50ml curaçao
Cointreau

### FOR THE CRÊPES

Whisk the flour, sugar, salt, eggs and a third of the milk in a bowl to a smooth batter.
Gradually stir in the rest of the milk and 50ml water. Leave the batter to rest in a
warm place for about an hour.

Brush a small 18–20cm frying pan with a little of the butter and place over a medium
heat. Add a ladleful of the batter and tilt the pan to cover the base thinly; cook the
crêpe for a minute on each side. Transfer the crêpe to a plate and repeat, stacking the
crêpes between sheets of greaseproof paper, until all the batter has been used up.

### FOR THE SAUCE

In a bowl, cream the butter with a spatula, then beat in the sugar, mandarin juice and
curaçao. Spread the mixture over the crêpes, fold into quarters and return to a frying
pan. Sprinkle with some sugar, liberally douse in Cointreau and flambé with a
blowtorch, being careful not to singe your moustache. Place on a serving dish and
serve warm.

# COFFEE BEAN PANNA COTTA, ESPRESSO SYRUP

ANT POWER

This dessert is very easy to make and can be made the day before a dinner party. It also serves as a great substitute for coffee after the meal, which, unless you have an espresso machine, can be a hassle – and no one likes bad coffee.

## SERVES 6

2 leaves of gelatin (available in most supermarkets)
150ml double cream
150ml milk
50g sugar
25g fresh coffee beans
20ml glucose (available from most supermarkets)
50g sugar
150ml very strong coffee

## TO SERVE

Biscotti or shortbread biscuits
Good-quality dark chocolate, finely grated
Strawberries (optional)

In a bowl, soak the gelatin with a little cold water. Place the cream, milk, sugar and coffee beans in a saucepan, and on a low heat slowly bring to the boil. Then remove from the heat and allow to infuse for 30 minutes.

Squeeze the water from the gelatin and add the softened leaves to the cream mixture, stirring thoroughly. Strain through a sieve and pour into small moulds or pots. Set in the fridge for at least 3 hours.

To make the syrup, place the glucose, sugar and coffee in a saucepan and reduce over a low heat until thick and syrupy. Set aside until serving. (If you put the syrup in the fridge, make sure you take it out a few hours before your meal so it warms to room temperature and softens to a thick syrup.)

## TO SERVE

Remove the panna cottas from their moulds or pots by inverting over a plate. Sprinkle on some grated chocolate, drizzle the syrup around the panna cottas and serve with biscotti or shortbread biscuits and strawberries.

# STEAMED MAPLE, LEMON AND BLACKBERRY PUDDING

**FRED SMITH**

## SERVES 6

300g butter
300g sugar
6 large free-range eggs
300g self-raising flour
75g stem ginger
Zest of 2 large lemons
Maple syrup
1 punnet of blackberries
Double cream to serve

Cream the butter and sugar in a mixing bowl. Then add the eggs, one at a time, followed by the flour, ginger and lemon zest, until you have a thick batter. Put to one side.

Preheat the oven to 180°C/gas mark 4. Place a generous dash of maple syrup and 3 or 4 blackberries in the bottom of 6 greased dariole moulds (or similar). Spoon the batter over the blackberries until the moulds are two-thirds full.

Loosely cover the moulds with tin foil and place in a roasting tray. Pour hot water into the tray so that it comes halfway up the moulds. Bake for 45 minutes.

To serve, remove the puddings from their moulds by inverting on a plate, and pour over the double cream.

# ROASTED FRUIT PARCELS WITH VANILLA ICE CREAM

## CIARAN MCGONAGLE

### SERVES 6

1 loaf of brioche (you can buy
this from a good bakery)
2 bananas, sliced
500g strawberries, hulled
3 peaches, halved
Brown sugar
Tub of vanilla ice cream

Light up your barbecue or preheat the oven to 180°C/gas mark 4. Cut the brioche
into 2cm thick slices and divide evenly between 6 x 15cm square sheets of tin foil
to form parcels. Evenly divide the bananas, strawberries and peaches between the
parcels and sprinkle with brown sugar. Close the foil parcels and cook on the
barbecue with the lid closed on a very low heat for about 30 minutes or in the
preheated oven for around 15 minutes.

### TO SERVE

Serve hot with vanilla ice cream.

**'THERE IS NO LOVE SINCERER
THAN THE LOVE OF FOOD'**

**GEORGE BERNARD SHAW**

# LEMON POSSET BRÛLEÉ

## IVAN VARIAN

Make this the day before as it needs to be in the fridge overnight to set.
A cook's blowtorch also comes in very handy for this recipe.

## SERVES 6

600ml double cream
150g caster sugar, plus a bit
extra for dusting
Juice and zest of 2 lemons

Get a big pan (much bigger than you think you need), pour in the cream and put on a high heat. Stir in the sugar until it has dissolved. Bring to the boil and simmer for 3 minutes. The cream will swell up in volume considerably and you'll soon discover if your pan is big enough. Once the 3 minutes are up, take it off the heat and stir in your lemon juice and zest. Pour into individual ramekins or something similar and place in the fridge overnight. The next day they should be set. If they're not, leave in the fridge a bit longer.

### TO SERVE

About 10 minutes before serving, dust a good coating of caster sugar on top of each posset and then fire up your blowtorch. Pass the flame over the top of the posset – the caster sugar should start to bubble and darken. Once it has, ease off on the flame and the top should form a lovely glassy shell. Repeat on each posset and serve.

If you don't have a cook's blowtorch, or for some reason you do not possess the masculine penchant for flame, then after you've dusted your possets with sugar, you can place them under the grill at its highest setting until the sugar starts to bubble and darken. Just be really careful when you serve them to your guests, as the porcelain will be extremely hot.

# COCONUT AND COINTREAU SORBET

## SIMON FERNANDEZ

This is one of those recipes that will impress your dinner guests for very little work indeed! It has an amazing combination of flavours, and is a really light finish to a meal.

### SERVES 6

130g caster sugar
250ml coconut milk
150ml coconut water (available from most supermarkets)
Juice of ½ lime, plus zest to garnish
50ml Cointreau
Mint leaves to garnish

In a saucepan over a medium heat, add the sugar, coconut milk and coconut water and stir until the sugar has dissolved. Take off the heat and allow to cool completely. Then add the lime juice and the Cointreau and mix thoroughly.

Pour the liquid into a couple of ice cube trays and put in the freezer. Once frozen, pop out the sorbet cubes, put them in a food processor and run the motor until you have a slushy consistency. Refreeze immediately in a Tupperware container.

### TO SERVE

Put a couple of good-sized scoops in a decorative cup or a Martini glass. Sprinkle on a few strands of lime zest and place a mint leaf in the centre of each sorbet. Serve immediately.

# COOK SAUCES, CHUTNEYS AND JAMS

# TOMATO, CHILLI AND MUSTARD MAN JAM

**MARTIN DOREY**

This is a proper man jam for proper Mo-wearing men. Chutney makes life better. It's an extra dash of pizzazz that can make dull food sing, make a boring sandwich come to life and turn a dreary burger into a griddle pan masterpiece. The Movember Man Jam is fruity and spicy. Just the way you like it. Just the way my dad would have liked it, were he here today. We lost him to prostate cancer in 2006.

### MAKES ABOUT A JAR

6 ripe tomatoes
1 red onion, peeled and finely chopped
1 red pepper, chopped
1 red chilli, finely chopped
½ teaspoon turmeric
1 teaspoon wholegrain mustard
2 sprigs of fresh rosemary
100ml white wine vinegar
100g organic caster sugar
1 teaspoon salt
Vegetable oil

Peel and deseed the tomatoes. (Removing the skin is easy if you soak them in boiling water for 2 minutes then plunge them in cold water for 1 minute.) Sweat the red onion in a little vegetable oil for a few minutes. Then add the tomatoes, pepper, chilli, turmeric, mustard and rosemary. Simmer gently for about 40 minutes or until the tomatoes are reduced to a pulp. Add the vinegar, sugar and salt, and simmer until all the liquid has evaporated (about 15–20 minutes). Cool, empty into a sterilised jar and keep in the fridge for up to 1 month.

**See page 13 for tips on how to sterilise jars and bottles.**

'IT'S BEEN A CHALLENGE – I TRIED TO GROW A MO FOR 30 DAYS BUT BEING A BIT FAIR AND FRECKLY, THE ODDS ARE STACKED AGAINST ME. I'VE HEARD THERE IS A MOVEMBER CATEGORY CALLED LAME-MO?'
**MARTIN DOREY**

# FIG CHUTNEY

### DEON JANSEN

A perfect partner with cheese or any kind of terrine.

10 figs, chopped
75g shallots, peeled and finely diced
175g sugar
125ml white wine
125ml white wine vinegar
1 teaspoon five-spice powder
1 teaspoon cinnamon
½ star anise

Put everything in a saucepan and gently heat, stirring until the sugar dissolves. Then gently bubble for 30 minutes until the figs and shallots are softened and the chutney has thickened slightly. Spoon into a sterilised jar.

# RED PEPPER AND ROSEMARY PESTO

### DEON JANSEN

Great with lamb chops or any farm animal.

125g pine nuts
200ml olive oil
4 red bell peppers, deseeded and diced
3 garlic cloves, peeled and chopped
½ bunch of rosemary, leaves picked
A bunch of basil, picked
125g grated Parmesan
Juice of 1 lemon
A pinch of salt and pepper

Toast the pine nuts by dry-frying in a small frying pan for a few minutes until golden, shaking the pan often. Heat the oil in a large saucepan and over a gentle heat, sauté the peppers, garlic and rosemary until the peppers are tender. Transfer to a food processor and whizz until smooth. Add the basil and pine nuts and pulse briefly, then stir in the rest of the ingredients. Keep in the fridge in a sterilised jar.

# MOHUMRA

### ANT POWER

This can be served as a dip with flatbread or with barbecue meat.

8 red peppers
500ml olive oil
8 garlic cloves, peeled
100g breadcrumbs
2 tablespoons cumin
1 tablespoon chilli flakes
1 tablespoon ground black pepper
150g walnuts, toasted
Juice of 4 lemons
2 tablespoons brown sugar
1 tablespoon sumac
1 teaspoon smoked paprika

In a hot oven or on the barbecue, roast the peppers until blistered and charred. Place in a large bowl and cover with cling film – the steam will help the skin to separate and make them easy to peel when cool. When cool enough to touch, peel, deseed and transfer to a blender. Blitz, remove and set aside in a bowl.

Heat the oil in a large saucepan and gently cook the garlic cloves over a low heat. When golden, add the breadcrumbs, cumin, chilli flakes and black pepper. Remove from the heat, transfer to a blender and blitz with the walnuts, lemon juice, sugar, sumac and smoked paprika. Transfer to the bowl with the peppers and mix well. Keep in the fridge for up to 3 days in a covered bowl.

# ONION JAM

### ANT POWER

Great with everything!

4 tablespoons olive oil
4 large onions, peeled and finely sliced
100g sugar
50ml orange juice
½ cinnamon stick
2 garlic cloves, peeled and finely diced
A few sprigs of thyme
1 bay leaf
1 tablespoon mustard seeds, roasted
A pinch of salt and pepper
50ml port
125ml red wine

In a heavy-based saucepan, heat the oil and add the onions. Sweat over a low heat until the onions are a golden colour. Add the sugar, orange juice, cinnamon, garlic, thyme, bay leaf, mustard seeds and salt and pepper. Cook for 15 minutes until the onions are starting to caramelise. Add the port and wine and cook over a low heat for 30 minutes or until the onions are sticky like jam.

# BEETROOT TAPENADE

### ANT POWER

A great accompaniment to beef but also works well with salmon.

500g grated beetroot
100g grated fresh horseradish
40ml raspberry vinegar (or use all red wine vinegar)
25ml red wine vinegar
50ml olive oil
Salt and pepper

Mix all the ingredients together.

# CHIMICHURRI

### ANT POWER

A bunch of parsley
A bunch of oregano
½ bunch of coriander
1 teaspoon dried chilli flakes
4 red chillies, deseeded
3 shallots, peeled
8 garlic cloves, peeled
1 tablespoon smoked paprika
1 teaspoon cumin
600ml extra-virgin olive oil
100ml sherry vinegar
Salt and pepper

Put everything in a blender and blitz until you have a coarse mixture.

# CUCUMBER PICKLE

### ANT POWER

Awesome with barbecues or spicy curries.

100g sesame seeds
2 cucumbers
50g table salt
2 spring onions, chopped
1 garlic clove, peeled and crushed
30g sugar
50ml sesame oil
75ml rice wine vinegar
1 chilli, deseeded and chopped
Juice of 2 lemons

Dry-fry the sesame seeds in a small frying pan for few minutes until golden, shaking the pan often. Cut the cucumbers lengthways and use a spoon to scrape out the seeds. Then thinly slice at an angle and sprinkle on the salt, making sure the cucumbers are well covered. Leave for an hour, then wash thoroughly to remove all the salt. (This will draw out excess moisture from the cucumbers so the finished product isn't soggy). Mix all the ingredients together and let infuse over 24 hours.

# TOMATO JAM

### SAM WILSON

Great on seafood, killer on a burger or a steak sandwich.

500g plum tomatoes, cored and chopped
125g sugar
2 tablespoons lime juice
¼ teaspoon ground cinnamon
¼ teaspoon allspice
½ teaspoon ground cumin
½ teaspoon sea salt
½ teaspoon ground black pepper
1 dried chilli, crumbled

Place all the ingredients in a pan and bring to the boil. Then turn the temperature down and simmer, stirring occasionally, until the tomatoes have dissolved and the jam is thick and glossy. This should take 45 minutes and the jam can be stored in the fridge for 2 weeks.

# SAUCE VIERGE

### SAM WILSON

A tangy warm dressing that is great with a piece of sea bass.

10 garlic cloves, peeled and finely chopped
3 shallots, peeled and finely chopped
375ml olive oil
10 tomatoes, cut into quarters and deseeded
50ml white wine vinegar
1 bunch of tarragon, chopped
1½ bunch of basil, chopped
200g pitted olives
Salt and pepper

Put the garlic, shallots and olive oil in a saucepan and cook on a low heat for 3 minutes or until just softened. Add the tomatoes, vinegar, tarragon, basil and olives, and season to taste. This will keep for a few weeks in the fridge.

# DUKKA SPICE

### SAM WILSON

North African dukka spice mix is amazing on just about anything. Make a big batch and keep in the cupboard, as you will use it!

175g sesame seeds
40g coriander seeds
60g hazelnuts, peeled
10g cumin

Put all the ingredients, except the cumin, in a frying pan and gently heat. When they are toasted and smelling delicious, transfer to a blender and blitz lightly. Mix together with the cumin.

# CHILLI SWEETCORN SALSA

### SAM WILSON

Goes with steak, burgers and just about anything barbecued.

6 sweetcorn cobs
2 red peppers, deseeded and diced into the size of sweetcorn kernels
2 red chillies, deseeded and finely diced
10g Spanish smoked paprika
A bunch of coriander, chopped
Salt and pepper to taste
Sherry vinegar to taste

In a pan of boiling water, cook the sweetcorn cobs for 8 minutes until almost tender. Then remove and roast on a hot griddle pan or barbecue for about 5 minutes for extra smokiness. Cut off the kernels from the cob, then mix with all the other ingredients.

## GRILLED LAMB RUB

### DAVE JOHNSON

Rub this on your meat a few
hours before your barbecue.

60g ginger, peeled and finely chopped
2 chillies, deseeded and chopped
15g ground cumin
12g paprika
7g turmeric
7g cinnamon
2 garlic cloves, peeled and crushed
½ bunch of coriander, chopped
7g cumin seeds
50ml olive oil

Gently cook the ingredients in the
olive oil for 2 minutes, then place in a
blender and blitz to a smooth paste.

## ALMOND AIOLI

### DAVE JOHNSON

Great with grilled fish and
chicken

100g whole blanched almonds
4 garlic cloves, peeled
A pinch of salt
Lemon juice to taste
4 egg yolks
500ml olive oil
500ml vegetable oil
Salt and pepper

Toast the almonds in a frying pan
over a low heat until golden. Cool,
roughly chop and put aside. Crush
the garlic with the salt in a pestle and
mortar. When you have a smooth
paste, add the lemon juice, transfer to
a mixing bowl, add the egg yolks and
whisk in the olive and vegetable oils
slowly. Stir in the chopped almonds
and season to taste.

## APPLE AND HORSERADISH YOGURT

### TROY MAGUIRE

Good with smoked mackerel or
smoked trout.

1–3 tablespoons grated horseradish root
(depending on how hot you like it)
200g natural plain yogurt
1 apple, peeled, cored and finely diced
Salt and pepper

In a bowl, mix the horseradish with
the yogurt. Leave for a day to infuse
in the fridge. Then pass through a
sieve to remove the horseradish bits,
add the diced apple and a touch of
seasoning. Keep in the fridge for up
to 3 days.

## PEAR MUSTARD

### TROY MAGUIRE

A perfect partner with cooked
hams, cheeses and cold meats.

250g sugar
4 pears, halved and cored
Wholegrain mustard

Put the sugar and 250ml cold water
in a saucepan. Gently heat, stirring
until the sugar has dissolved. Add the
pears, bring to a simmer, cover and
cook for 10–20 minutes until tender
(this will depend on the ripeness of
the pears). Then whizz in a blender
until puréed. Weigh the pear purée
and add an equal amount of
wholegrain mustard. Keep in the
fridge for up to 5 days.

# THE PERSONA OF
# A MAN WITH A MO

He has an air of sociability and hospitality

———

He is unrushed, calm and always has time

———

He is in control of his life, and never stressed

———

He is naturally charming to everyone he meets

———

He rarely loses his temper and never in public

———

He can seemingly handle any situation that is thrown at him

———

He is patient, and left unruffled by life's daily irritations

———

He is modest, yet confident, and cultivates an air of ease

# INDEX

aioli
  almond 183
  saffron 150
almonds
  almond aioli 183
  almond couscous 124–5
  Baked apples with crème fraîche 160–1
  salsa agresto 154
apples
  Apple and horseradish yogurt 183
  Baked apples with crème fraîche 160–1
  Seared river trout with apple purée, herbed
    fennel salad and salsa agresto 154–5
  Warm pigeon breast salad with caramelised
    apple, crispy chorizo and balsamic syrup
    32–3
Arroz al horno with fresh tomato sauce 92–3
artichokes, Elwy Valley lamb and liver with
  artichokes, baby beets and wild mushrooms
  98–9
asparagus
  Arroz al horno with fresh tomato sauce 92–3
  Asparagus, soft duck egg, crispy ham and
    shaved parmesan 62–3
  Grilled whole black bream, Tuscan
    potatoes, asparagus and salsa verde
    140–1
  Roasted salmon, samphire, asparagus and
    cherry tomatoes with lemon dill dressing
    146–7
avocados
  Spiced crab and avocado on toast 44–5
  Sustainable white fish ceviche with
    edamame beans 136–7

bacon
  Roast pheasant with Savoy cabbage, chicory
    and crispy pancetta 130–1
Baked apples with crème fraîche 160–1
Baked cheese with winter herbs 48–9
bananas, Roasted fruit parcels with vanilla ice
  cream 172–3
barbecues 79
  Chermoula chicken, tabbouleh,
    good times 76–7
  Chilli squid, Thai basil watermelon salad,
    chilli caramel 82–3
  Davis family pork ribs 86–7
  Grilled Cornish squid salad, chilli and
    grape gremolata 80–1
  Pork chops with warm roast pumpkin,
    beetroot, spinach, lentil and red pepper
    salad 72–3
  Prawns with piri piri 84–5
  Roasted fruit parcels with vanilla ice

cream 172–3
  Rump of beef, beetroot and feta and potato
    salad 74–5
beans *see* edamame beans; green beans
Beaufort cheese 52
beef
  Barbecued rump of beef, beetroot and feta
    and potato salad 74–5
  Beef bourguignon, potato and parsnip
    mash 100–1
  Peat-roasted organic beef fillet 116–17
  Raw beef, capers, chicory and pickled
    walnuts 30–1
  Thai beef salad 26–7
beer, Mussels cooked in 58–9
beetroot
  Barbecued rump of beef, beetroot and feta
    and potato salad 74–5
  Barbecued pork chops with warm roast
    pumpkin, beetroot, spinach, lentil
    and red pepper salad 72–3
  Beetroot tapenade 181
  Elwy Valley lamb and liver with artichokes,
    baby beets and wild mushrooms
    98–9
black bream, Grilled whole, Tuscan potatoes,
  grilled asparagus and salsa verde 140–1
blackberries, Steamed maple, lemon and
  blackberry pudding 170–1
blinis, Whitefish roe mousse 56–7
Blueberry and Victoria plum crumble, mint
  yogurt 164–5
Brazil nut and pumpkin seed loaf 18
bread
  Brazil nut and pumpkin seed loaf 18
  'Real' bread dough focaccia 66–7
  'Real' bread dough pizza 68–9
  Roast loin of lamb in bread 112–13
  Roasted fruit parcels with vanilla ice cream
    172–3
bream *see* black bream; sea bream
brioche, Roasted fruit parcels with vanilla ice
  cream 172–3
bulgur wheat, tabbouleh 76
butternut squash, Barbecued pork chops with
  warm roast pumpkin, beetroot, spinach,
  lentil and red pepper salad 72–3

cabbage, Roast pheasant with Savoy cabbage,
  chicory and crispy pancetta 130–1
capers, Raw beef, capers, chicory and pickled
  walnuts 30–1
cappuccino, Wild mushroom, wild mushroom
  croustades 46–7
Cauliflower soup with sherry tapenade 20–1
cavolo nero, Rabbit ballotine 54–5
ceviche, Sustainable white fish ceviche with

edamame beans 136–7
Chanterelle-filled reindeer fillet with cranberry
  sauce 118–19
cheese
  Baked cheese with winter herbs 48–9
  Cheese fondue 52–3
Chermoula spring chicken, grilled Romero
  peppers, almond couscous, coriander Greek
  yogurt 124–5
chicken
  Barbecued chermoula chicken, tabbouleh,
    good times 76–7
  Chermoula spring chicken, grilled Romero
    peppers, almond couscous,
    coriander Greek yogurt 124–5
  Chicken with morel mushrooms 126–7
  Chicken pie, mash and green beans 128–9
chicory
  Raw beef, capers, chicory and pickled
    walnuts 30–1
  Roast pheasant with savoy cabbage, chicory
    and crispy pancetta 130–1
Chilled watercress soup, prawns, chilli crème
  fraîche 24–5
chillies
  Barbecued prawns with piri piri 84
  Barbecued chilli squid, Thai basil
    watermelon salad, chilli caramel 82–3
  Chilli jam 58
  Chilli sweetcorn salsa 185
  Chimichurri 184
  Grilled Cornish squid salad with chilli and
    grape gremolata 80
  Roasted chilli paste 91
  Tomato, chilli and mustard man jam 180
Chimichurri 184
chocolate, Rabbit with snails and chocolate
  106–7
chorizo
  Rabbit with snails and chocolate 106–7
  Warm pigeon breast salad with caramelised
    apple, crispy chorizo and balsamic
    syrup 32–3
chutneys
  Fig chutney 181
  *see also* jams; pickles
cockles, Grilled sardine fillets provençal 138–9
Coconut and Cointreau sorbet 176–7
coconut cream
  Mussels cooked in beer with chilli jam 58
  Sustainable white fish ceviche with
    edamame beans 136–7
coconut milk
  Coconut and Cointreau sorbet 176–7
  Thai Lon of pork and prawn with grilled sea
    bass 94–5
Coffee bean panna cotta, espresso syrup 168–9

Comté cheese 52
courgettes, Grilled sardine fillets provençal 138–9
couscous
    almond 124–5
    pomegranate 96
crab, Spiced crab and avocado on toast 44–5
cranberries, Chanterelle-filled reindeer fillet with cranberry sauce 118–19
crayfish 120–1
Crêpes Suzette 166–7
croustades, Wild mushroom cappuccino, wild mushroom 46–7
crumble, Blueberry and Victoria plum crumble, mint yogurt 164–5
cucumber, Cucumber pickle 182

Davis family pork ribs 86–7
dinner parties 35, 38–9
dressings
    lemon and chive 28
    lemon dill 146
dry spice mix, Davis family pork ribs 87
Dukka spice 182

edamame beans, Sustainable white fish ceviche with 136–7
eggs
    Asparagus, soft duck egg, crispy ham and shaved parmesan 62–3
    Smoked haddock risotto, soft boiled quail eggs, parsnip crisps 152–3
elderberry yogurt, Lettuce wraps with pheasant, fried onions and 64–5
Elwy Valley lamb and liver with artichokes, baby beets and wild mushrooms 98–9
Emmental cheese 52
equipment 10–11
essential fatty acids 8, 28

fennel
    fennel purée 99
    Fish stew with snapper, monkfish, braised fennel and saffron aioli 150–1
    Salt crust baked wild sea bream 142–3
    Seared river trout with apple purée, herbed fennel salad and salsa agresto 154–5
feta cheese
    Barbecued rump of beef, beetroot and feta salad 74–5
    Warm roast pumpkin, beetroot, spinach, lentil and red pepper 72–3
Fig chutney 181
fish
    buying 13
    Fish stew with snapper, monkfish, braised fennel and saffron aioli 150–1

Grilled mackerel, Niçoise salad, lemon and chive dressing 28–9
Grilled sardine fillets provençal 138–9
Grilled whole black bream, Tuscan potatoes, grilled asparagus and salsa verde 140–1
Herb-crusted John Dory with a curried mussel broth 149
Poached trout, herb salad and mayonnaise 40–1
Roasted salmon, samphire, asparagus and cherry tomatoes with lemon dill dressing 146–7
Salmon sashimi and salmon sushi 156–7
Salt crust baked wild sea bream 142–3
Seared river trout with apple purée, herbed fennel salad and salsa agresto 154–5
Smoked haddock risotto, soft boiled quail eggs, parsnip crisps 152–3
Sustainable white fish ceviche with edamame beans 136–7
Thai Lon of pork and prawn with grilled sea bass 94–5
Whitefish roe mousse blinis 56–7
see also fish by type
focaccia, 'Real' bread dough 66–7
fruit and vegetables
    a balanced diet 8
    seasons 14

game see pheasant; pigeon; quail; rabbit; reindeer; venison
ginger, Steamed maple, lemon and blackberry pudding 170–1
grapes, Grilled Cornish squid salad with chilli and grape gremolata 80
gratin, leek and cep mushroom 115
green beans
    Arroz al horno with fresh tomato sauce 92–3
    Chicken pie, mash and green beans 128–9
gremolata, chilli and grape 80
grilled lamb rub 183
Grilled sardine fillets provençal 138–9
Grilled whole black bream, Tuscan potatoes, asparagus and salsa verde 140–1
guavas 9
Gubbeen cheese 48

haddock, Smoked haddock risotto, soft boiled quail eggs, parsnip crisps 152–3
ham
    Asparagus, soft duck egg, crispy ham and shaved parmesan 62–3
    Pigeon terrine 60–1
    Rabbit ballotine 54–5

hazelnuts
    Dukka spice 184
    Pan-fried quail with roasted pumpkin and hazelnuts 132–3
healthy eating 8–9
herb salad 40–1
horseradish, Apple and horseradish yogurt 183

jams
    Chilli jam 58
    Onion jam 181
    Tomato, chilli and mustard man jam 180
    Tomato jam 182
    see also chutneys; pickles
John Dory, Herb-crusted, with a curried mussel broth 149

kitchen tips 13
knives 10–11

labna, sumac 96
lamb
    Burying the lamb 110–11
    Elwy Valley lamb and liver with artichokes, baby beets and wild mushrooms 98–9
    Grilled lamb rub 183
    Lamb, pomegranate couscous and sumac labna 96–7
    Roast loin of lamb in bread 112–13
leeks, Slow-roast Tamworth suckling pig shoulder, roast baby vegetables, leek and cep mushroom gratin, boulangère potatoes 114–15
lemons
    Lemon posset brûlée 174–5
    Steamed maple, lemon and blackberry pudding 170–1
lentils, Barbecued pork chops with warm roast pumpkin, beetroot, spinach, lentil and red pepper salad 72–3
Lettuce wraps with pheasant, elderberry yogurt and fried onions 64–5
limes, Coconut and Cointreau sorbet 176–7
liver, Elwy Valley lamb and liver with artichokes, baby beets and wild mushrooms 98–9
lycopene 9

mackerel, Grilled, Niçoise salad, lemon and chive dressing 28–9
maple syrup, Steamed maple, lemon and blackberry pudding 170–1
marinades, chermoula 77, 124–5
mascarpone, Raspberry meringues, roasted peaches and vanilla 162–3
mayonnaise, Tarragon and mustard 73

meringues, Raspberry, roasted peaches and vanilla mascarpone 162–3
Mo Bro Chefs 7
Mohumra 181
monkfish, Fish stew with snapper, monkfish, braised fennel and saffron aioli 150–1
mousse, Whitefish roe 56–7
moustaches, foods to approach with caution 14
mushrooms
  Arroz al horno with fresh tomato sauce 92–3
  Chanterelle-filled reindeer fillet with cranberry sauce 118–19
  Chicken with morel mushrooms 126–7
  Elwy Valley lamb and liver with artichokes, baby beets and wild mushrooms 98–9
  Roast rabbit with crispy wild mushroom ravioli 104–5
  Slow-roast Tamworth suckling pig shoulder, roast baby vegetables, leek and cep mushroom gratin, boulangère potatoes 114–15
  Wild mushroom cappuccino, wild mushroom croustades 46–7
mussels
  Grilled sardine fillets provençal 138–9
  Herb-crusted John Dory with a curried mussel broth 149
  Mussels cooked in beer with chilli jam 58–9
mustard
  Pear mustard 183
  Tarragon and mustard mayonnaise 73
  Tomato, chilli and mustard man jam 180

Niçoise salad 28–9

onions, Lettuce wraps with pheasant, elderberry yogurt and fried 64–5
oranges, Crêpes Suzette 166–7
oysters, buying 13

Pan-fried quail with roasted pumpkin and hazelnuts 132–3
pancakes, Crêpes Suzette 166–7
panna cotta, Coffee bean, espresso syrup 168–9
papayas 9
  Som tam green papaya salad 36
Parma ham, Rabbit ballotine 54–5
parsnips
  parsnip crisps 153
  potato and parsnip mash 100
  Venison with charred sweetcorn, mashed potato, roast parsnips and port and redcurrant jus 102–3
peaches
  Raspberry meringues, roasted peaches and vanilla mascarpone 162–3

Roasted fruit parcels with vanilla ice cream 172–3
Pear mustard 183
peat
  cooking with 116
  Peat-roasted organic beef fillet 116–17
peppers see chillies; red peppers
pesto, Red pepper and rosemary 181
pheasant
  Lettuce wraps with pheasant, elderberry yogurt and fried onions 64–5
  Roast pheasant with Savoy cabbage, chicory and crispy pancetta 130–1
pickles
  Cucumber pickle 182
  see also chutneys; jams
pigeon
  Pigeon terrine 60–1
  Warm pigeon breast salad with caramelised apple, crispy chorizo and balsamic syrup 32–3
pink grapefruit 9
piri piri 84
pizza, 'Real' bread dough 68–9
plums
  Blueberry and Victoria plum crumble, mint yogurt 164–5
  Vine tomato and plum soup 18–19
Poached trout, herb salad and mayonnaise 40–1
pomegranate
  Pomegranate couscous 96
  Rabbit ballotine 54–5
pork
  Arroz al horno with fresh tomato sauce 92–3
  Barbecued pork chops with warm roast pumpkin, beetroot, spinach, lentil and red pepper salad 72–3
  Davis family pork ribs 86–7
  Pigeon terrine 60
  Roast pork belly stir-fry with roast chilli paste 90–1
  Slow-roast Tamworth suckling pig shoulder, roast baby vegetables, leek and cep mushroom gratin, boulangère potatoes 114–15
  Thai Lon of pork and prawn with grilled sea bass 94–5
port and redcurrant jus 103
potatoes
  Arroz al horno with fresh tomato sauce 92–3
  Beef bourguignon, potato and parsnip mash 100
  Boulangère 115
  Chicken pie, mash and green beans 128–9

potato salad 74
  Tuscan 141
  Venison with charred sweetcorn, mashed potato, roast parsnips and port and redcurrant jus 102–3
poultry see chicken
prawns
  Barbecued prawns with piri piri 84
  Chilled watercress soup, prawns, chilli crème fraîche 24–5
  Spicy tomato and red pepper soup, seared prawns, olive oil and chives 22–3
  Thai Lon of pork and prawn with grilled sea bass 94–5
pumpkin
  Barbecued pork chops with warm roast pumpkin, beetroot, spinach, lentil and red pepper salad 72–3
  Pan-fried quail with roasted pumpkin and hazelnuts 132–3
pumpkin seeds, Brazil nut and pumpkin seed loaf 18

quail, Pan-fried, with roasted pumpkin and hazelnuts 132–3

rabbit
  Rabbit ballotine 54–5
  Rabbit with snails and chocolate 106–7
  Roast rabbit with crispy wild mushroom ravioli 104–5
Raspberry meringues, roasted peaches and vanilla mascarpone 162–3
ravioli, Roast rabbit with crispy wild mushroom 104–5
Raw beef, capers, chicory and pickled walnuts 30–1
red peppers
  Barbecued pork chops with warm roast pumpkin, beetroot, spinach, lentil and red pepper salad 72–3
  Chermoula spring chicken, grilled Romero peppers, almond couscous, coriander Greek yogurt 124–5
  Chilli sweetcorn salsa 183
  Mohumra 181
  Red pepper and rosemary pesto 181
  Spicy tomato and red pepper soup, seared prawns, olive oil and chives 22–3
redcurrants, port and redcurrant jus 103
reindeer, Chanterelle-filled reindeer fillet with cranberry sauce 118–19
rice
  Arroz al horno with fresh tomato sauce 92–3
  Smoked haddock risotto, soft boiled quail eggs, parsnip crisps 152–3

Roast loin of lamb in bread 112–13
Roast pheasant with Savoy cabbage, chicory and crispy pancetta 130–1
Roast pork belly stir-fry with roast chilli paste 90–1
Roast rabbit with crispy wild mushroom ravioli 104–5
Roasted fruit parcels with vanilla ice cream 172–3
Roasted salmon, samphire, asparagus and cherry tomatoes with lemon dill dressing 146–7

salads
    beetroot and feta 74–5
    Grilled Cornish squid salad, chilli and grape gremolata 80–1
    Grilled mackerel, Niçoise salad, lemon and chive dressing 28–9
    Poached trout, herb salad and mayonnaise 40–1
    potato 74
    Raw beef, capers, chicory and pickled walnuts 30–1
    Seared river trout with apple purée, herbed fennel salad and salsa agresto 154–5
    Som tam green papaya 36
    Thai basil watermelon 82–3
    Thai beef 26–7
    Warm pigeon breast salad with caramelised apple, crispy chorizo and balsamic syrup 32–3
    Warm roast pumpkin, beetroot, spinach, lentil and red pepper 72–3
salmon
    Roasted salmon, samphire, asparagus and cherry tomatoes with lemon dill dressing 146–7
    Salmon sashimi and salmon sushi 156–7
salsa
    agresto 154
    Chilli sweetcorn 182
    verde 141
Salt crust baked wild sea bream 142–3
samphire, Roasted salmon, samphire, asparagus and cherry tomatoes with lemon dill dressing 146–7
sardines, Grilled sardine fillets provençal 138–9
sashimi, Salmon sashimi and salmon sushi 156–7
Sauce vierge 138, 182
sausages
    Arroz al horno with fresh tomato sauce 92–3
    Rabbit with snails and chocolate 106–7
    Warm pigeon breast salad with caramelised apple, crispy chorizo and balsamic

syrup 32–3
sea bass, Thai Lon of pork and prawn with grilled 94–5
sea bream, Salt crust baked wild 142–3
Seared river trout with apple purée, herbed fennel salad and salsa agresto 154–5
sesame seeds, Dukka spice 182
shellfish see cockles; crab; crayfish; mussels; oysters; prawns; squid;
sherry tapenade 21
shopping tips 13
Slow-roast Tamworth suckling pig shoulder, roast baby vegetables, leek and cep mushroom gratin, boulangère potatoes 114–15
Smoked haddock risotto, soft boiled quail eggs, parsnip crisps 152–3
snails, Rabbit with snails and chocolate 106–7
snapper, Fish stew with snapper, monkfish, braised fennel and saffron aioli 150–1
Som tam green papaya salad 36
sorbets, Coconut and Cointreau 176–7
soups
    Cauliflower soup with sherry tapenade 20–1
    Chilled watercress soup, prawns, chilli crème fraîche 24–5
    Spicy tomato and red pepper soup, seared prawns, olive oil and chives 22–3
    Vine tomato and plum 18–19
Spiced crab and avocado on toast 44–5
Spicy tomato and red pepper soup, seared prawns, olive oil and chives 22–3
spinach, Barbecued pork chops with warm roast pumpkin, beetroot, spinach, lentil and red pepper salad 72–3
squid
    Barbecued chilli squid, Thai basil watermelon salad, chilli caramel 82–3
    Grilled Cornish squid salad, chilli and grape gremolata 80–1
Steamed maple, lemon and blackberry pudding 170–1
store cupboard ingredients 14
strawberries, Roasted fruit parcels with vanilla ice cream 172–3
sumac labna 96
sushi, Salmon sashimi and salmon sushi 156–7
Sustainable white fish ceviche with edamame beans 136–7
sweetcorn
    Chilli sweetcorn salsa 183
    Venison with charred sweetcorn, mashed potato, roast parsnips and port and redcurrant jus 102–3

tabbouleh 76

tapenade 138
    beetroot 181
    sherry 21
terrines, Pigeon 60–1
Thai basil watermelon salad 82–3
Thai beef salad 26–7
Thai Lon of pork and prawn with grilled sea bass 94–5
tomatoes
    Arroz al horno with fresh tomato sauce 92–3
    Health properties 9
    Roasted salmon, samphire, asparagus and cherry tomatoes with lemon dill dressing 146–7
    Spicy tomato and red pepper soup, seared prawns, olive oil and chives 22–3
    Tomato, chilli and mustard man jam 180
    Tomato jam 182
    tomato sauce (for pizza) 68
    Vine tomato and plum soup 18–19
trout
    Poached trout, herb salad and mayonnaise 40–1
    Seared river trout with apple purée, herbed fennel salad and salsa agresto 154–5
Tuscan potatoes 141

Venison with charred sweetcorn, mashed potato, roast parsnips and port and redcurrant jus 102–3
Vine tomato and plum soup 18–19
vinegar, elderberry 64

walnuts
    Mohumra 181
    Raw beef, capers, chicory and pickled 30–1
    salsa agresto 154
watercress, Chilled watercress soup, prawns, chilli crème fraîche 24–5
watermelons 9
    Thai basil watermelon salad 82–3
Whitefish roe mousse blinis 56–7
Wild mushroom cappuccino, wild mushroom croustades 46–7

yogurt
    Apple and horseradish 183
    coriander Greek 124–5
    elderberry 64–5
    mint 164

# MOUSTACHE RESPECT

This here Movember cookbook is a compilation of three fine publications created by a dedicated team of Mo crew that give their heart, Mo and soul to Movember. To our master chefs and taste engineers who contributed to this book, we can't thank you enough for letting us into the world of your culinary minds, kitchens, families, homes and restaurants.

To our foragers and modern day hunter-gatherers, for seeking Mother Nature's forbidden fruit – picking mushrooms, finding fish and hunting game. You have opened our eyes to so many new flavours and inspired us all.

To our agency TASTE PR for helping us unearth flavour pioneers, foodies, chefs and foragers from far and wide, and for fearlessly following us across the country in what have been some magic moments.

To our resident chef, ink slinger and Baron of Beef Ant Power, who has shared knowledge and brought the world of fine food to the moustache with passion and precision. Ant has been instrumental in setting the standard of Movember dishes; helping gather together chefs from across the land into one collaborative piece and stamping our Movember feel and twist on what we are proud to call our own journey with food.

To our image-maker and photo taker Steve Ryan who has helped shape our Movember food aesthetic. Steve has a never-ending commitment to capturing a true Mo moment since way back for Movember, going above and beyond in the quest for the perfect light.

To our proofreaders for their endless candlelit nights spent pouring over these words, making sure the chefs' poetic licenses are still in date and the recipes read as well as they taste.

To Alex Denman for artfully assembling all our ideas, recipes and images into a visual feast for Mo Bros with the Urchin crew and Mark Calderbank design partner-in-crime.

To our literary agent Jonathan Conway and also to Cindy Chan, Jon Butler and everyone at our publishers Macmillan, for taking the chance on some guys who just want to hunt, slice, grill, eat and experience food at its best with our crews.

To the animals that died for the cause. Never was so much owed by so many to so few. (W. Churchill)

And to the Movember roadies, the heavy lifters, the ringmasters and purveyors of knowledge that helped make the cookbooks happen. Your passion and commitment year in, year out to bring these flavours to life is unprecedented – you all know who you are and it doesn't go unnoticed.

To the Mo Bros and Mo Sistas for trusting us to give them tasty recipes to fill their homes with people, flavour and fun.

Movember wouldn't exist without all of you. We salute you.

'FOR EVERY MEAL THAT PASSES A MOUSTACHED LIP, WE ARE TRULY GRATEFUL'

DAVE BONE